*Thanks 4 giving it your a[ll]*
*Ron N Plum*
*"Boo!"*

## Haunted Toys

# Haunted Toys
## by David Weatherly & Ross Allison

Copyright © 2017 Leprechaun Productions
All Rights Reserved

No part of the primary content of this publication may be reproduced or transmitted in any form or by any means, mechanical or electronic, including photocopying and recording, or by any information storage and retrieval system, without permission in writing from author or publisher (except by a reviewer, who may quote brief passages and/or show brief video clips in review.) Forms included within this publication for research documentation and sketches may be reproduced by the original purchaser for individual use.

ISBN 10 - 978-1-945950-02-5

Published by:

**Leprechaun Productions**
**Nevada • Texas**

Cover by: Ross Allison

Back cover image by: June Antoinette Nixon

Editor: A. Dale Triplett

Book layout and photo illustrations by: SMAK
www.smakgraphics.com

Printed in the United States of America

David would like to dedicate his portion of this book:

To my children with love and affection
May your lives always be filled with wonder and beauty

Ross would like to dead☠icate his part of the book:

To my nieces
Emily, Ashlynn and Riana
May all your dreams come true

# Editor's Note

Images can often tell us a story far better than any text or prose. The perfect picture can lead our imagination to deeper light on the accompanying text — perhaps even when the image isn't necessarily a true reflection of the original content. *Haunted Toys* is rife with delightfully creepy images rendered by the creative imagination of the artist. Some are of the various toys described, but most are simply meant to paint a picture of intent, a visual temptation of your imagination's taste buds. None are meant to disparage or directly represent the actual toys described or their owners, nor should they in any way be misconstrued as representative of trademarked items, goods or corporations. The images themselves are art, and are not themselves haunted… or are they? Let your dreams decide, and enjoy your play-time with all of these *Haunted Toys*.

- A. Dale Triplett

# Table of Contents

| | |
|---|---|
| Introduction | *ix* |
| Chapter 1 | *1* |
| Chapter 2 | *41* |
| Chapter 3 | *61* |
| Chapter 4 | *101* |
| About the Authors | *129* |

# Introduction:
# Why Haunted Toys?

Hollywood has certainly played with our imaginations when it comes to creepy dolls and toys. That famous red-headed doll "Chucky" undoubtedly loved to play with sharp objects, and let's not forget that scary clown from the movie Poltergeist hiding under your bed. These horrifying tales didn't start in tinseltown, though. Creepy dolls have been frightening folks for a long, long time.

The first reported haunted doll goes clear back to the Egyptians. It is said that those whom had it out for Ramses III attempted to use wax-like figures made in his likeness to bring about his death. These figures would come to life and curse anyone they resembled. Many of these relics used in rituals or for ceremonial purposes were also known as poppets, effigies and voodoo dolls. Different cultures had various reasons for using effigies, some were even used to drive evil from the body or to absorb your soul.

So it's no wonder these troubling stories stir up our fears when confronted by any crusty old doll that stares you down. Is there something lurking behind those glass eyes? Or is it just a toy?

For years the curious have wondered whether a spirit can possess an object, such as a toy or doll. Several believe it is entirely possible. A popular belief is these objects can hold energy within or around it that has been passed on to them.

For instance, certain toys seem to have the ability to calm or comfort a child for whatever reason. With genuine love and care that toy now becomes an essential part of the adolescent's life. The longer the child keeps the toy in his or her possession the more energy it receives. This relationship binds the two and in some cases, becomes an obsession that builds a stronger bond. Once this has transpired the toy then begins to take on a life of its own. And with some children this can happen almost immediately.

Think about it — the energy of an innocent youth can be extremely strong and focused, developing a curiosity of everything around them including the toy. But be warned, given what these toys can be exposed to throughout the child's life, negative and positive traits may pass on to the toy as well.

Some of the most heartbreaking stories of haunted toys are those of the ones left behind when a child dies, either suddenly or after suffering a long illness. Additionally, children suffering from depression, mental illness or abuse may trigger a more sinister kind of possession.

When it comes to a more negative vibe, it's believed the item could hold onto the negative energy because someone was killed with the object while in their possession, or something traumatic happened around the object of their affection.

## 3 Kinds of Haunted Objects

1. Objects that absorb energy from their previous owner.
2. Objects possessed by a spirit.
3. Objects cursed through a spiritual ritual.

## 5 Signs A Toy Is Possessed

1. Bad vibes - Trust your instincts when you encounter an object that gives you more than just the willies.

2. Suspicious origins – If you come across a toy, either handmade or you seem to have trouble tracing down its heritage, be cautious.

3. Reanimation – Are you discovering the toy is being misplaced or appearing in areas you know it wasn't left? Or is the toy moving without the help of batteries or a wind-up mechanism?

4. Suspicious sounds – Some toys feature sound characteristics; a music box, talking, or even beeping. Most of these need to be triggered in some way. So don't be surprised if these toys play by themselves. Some say you may even hear the sounds of children giggling or even crying — even when NO children are present.

5. Doing harm – If your toy is becoming a tripping hazard or you're finding strange bruises or cuts on yourself or on your children that can't be explained, then it's time to rid yourself of this toy right away.

## Batteries NOT Included

Toys have come a long way through the decades. They are more sophisticated, entertaining and usually require batteries. So it's not too shocking when modern spooky accounts include tales of children's toys operating on their own in the middle of the night.

Stories include such tales as a family witnessing a toy cell phone ringing throughout the night, waking everyone in the house, but stops ringing when anyone picks it up. Of course, only to start ringing again once the phone is left and the person steps away. Or when a remote-controlled car shoots across the room and almost runs over your feet. This happens while the kids are at school and you believe you are home alone. How about when you wake to hear your wife singing your baby to sleep on the baby monitor, only to roll over and find her still in bed with you, fast asleep? But most unique are the stories of the toys that come to life after you discover there are NO batteries to power them.

One woman's son had two trucks, one was a boom box truck, and the other was a fire truck. Both had gone off at the same time while her son was sleeping in his room. To activate these trucks, you have to push a button so the music and siren go off. When they did go off, again at the exact same moment, she couldn't get them to stop and decided to remove the batteries. She was shocked to find there were no batteries in either of the trucks.

Another story includes one family woken to the sounds of one of their son's teddy bears that would announce which foot or hand was being squeezed, "That was my right hand, that was my left foot." The bear was found sitting in the corner of the room, however, the bear had stopped once the parents opened the door and found their son fast asleep. Concerned the bear might start up again, they removed the batteries and went back to bed. The next morning during breakfast, the father handed his son the batteries and explained to their son what had happened the night before. Their son had a puzzled look on his face and replied, "those batteries have been dead for a long time." It seemed the past few months his bear had stopped working. The confused father went straight to his son's room, grabbed the bear and put the batteries in. He then squeezed the hands and feet only to find no response whatsoever.

All of these stories are true accounts, and there are tons of blogs where witnesses have reported such encounters with toys somehow doing their own thing. Now skeptics might say it's caused by toys shifting due to gravity or low batteries causing surges. And perhaps they're right. However, so many of these events have no explanation, no rhyme or reason. We just have to chalk them up to those possible paranormal encounters that haunt the unexpected.

# Introduction: Why Haunted Toys?

# Chapter 1:
# Haunted Dolls

## Robert The Doll

Robert Did It!

He's been blamed for car accidents, job loss, a wide range of health issues, broken bones and severe illnesses, divorces, and countless other misfortunes.

He's 111 years old and resides at the Fort East Martello Museum in Key West, Florida, and he's known far and wide as Robert the doll.

Robert stands forty inches tall and is dressed in a sailor's uniform. He has small, shoe button eyes and a rather spongy appearance. His worn face is only vaguely human and he has what many see as a smirk. He's covered with small nicks, the scars of age and time. He is stuffed with excelsior, or wood wool made of slivers cut from logs.

Robert originally belonged to Robert Eugene Otto, an eccentric Key West artist who came from a wealthy and prominent family. Young Robert received the doll as a gift for his fourth birthday. Upon receiving it, he gave the doll his name and declared that from that time forward, the doll would be called Robert and that he would go by his middle name, Eugene, or Gene for short. Gene and Robert were inseparable. As Gene's constant companion, Robert even had his own chair at the dinner table and each night, Robert slept beside Gene in his bed.

Museum curator Cori Convertito notes:

"What people really remember is what they would probably term as an unhealthy relationship with the doll. He brought it everywhere, he talked about it in the first person as if he weren't a doll, he was Robert. As in he is a live entity."

It wasn't long before the young Gene began to blame things on the doll. He would frequently state "Robert did it!" when trouble arose around him. Broken and missing items, rooms in disarray, it always seemed to be Robert's fault. But it wasn't a simple matter of Gene making excuses for his own misdeeds.

The boy's parents said they could hear their child at night, having conversations with Robert. Another voice would answer, as if Robert was also talking. The Otto's thought perhaps it was just their son, using a different voice to pretend the doll was speaking. As things got stranger over the years, they began to second-guess their assumption. There were also claims that whenever someone spoke badly about Gene in his presence, the doll's expression would change.

When Gene got older, he moved away from Florida and left Robert behind in the family home. Gene attended fine arts schools in both Chicago and New York. He traveled overseas, and while in Paris he met a Boston native named Annette Parker. She would become his wife. Annette was a renowned pianist and at one point gave a command performance for the King of England. The couple married in 1930 and eventually moved back to the states, living in New York for several years. Gene's mother became very ill and he convinced his wife to move to Key West. Annette wasn't happy about moving away from the big city.

The couple took up residence in a stately home known as "The Artist House." Robert the doll was reunited with Gene and was given his own room upstairs in the home's turret. The doll had his own furniture and toys built just for his size. Kids walking by the home would often see Robert sitting by the window in his rocking chair. They claimed the doll would move around to different windows, looking down on them and that it would appear and disappear. Many of them started going out of their way so they didn't have to walk near the house with the living doll.

Annette couldn't stand Robert. She felt Gene paid more attention to the doll than he did to her. After her husband passed away in 1974, Annette put Robert in a trunk and tried to forget about him.

Myrtle Reuter purchased the Artist House and by default, became Robert the doll's new caretaker. Robert was back on display and visitors to the home reported hearing footsteps above them in the attic, as well as someone giggling. After owning the Artist House for twenty years, Reuter decided she'd had more than enough of Robert the doll. She said besides the constant noises from the attic, Robert would move around the house on his own, so in 1994 she donated the doll to the East Martello museum in Key West.

Since Robert's arrival at the museum, much has been learned about his origins. Early legends said the doll was given to Gene for his fourth birthday by the family's Bahamian maid. It was said she cursed the doll using black magic, and this is what caused it to seemingly exhibit a life of its own.

In recent years researchers have worked hard to discover Robert's true history, and they have traced the origins of the doll back to the Steiff Company, the same toy maker that first manufactured the Teddy Bear in honor of Theodore Roosevelt. It's now believed Robert was never intended to be sold as a toy, instead likely made as part of a set of window display items, likely as a jester or clown.

The sailor suit Robert wears was not supplied by the company and may have been an outfit young Gene wore himself as a child. It was discovered the doll was purchased by the boy's grandfather on one of his trips to Germany, as a unique birthday present for young Gene.

Robert seems quite at home at the museum and has become a popular stop on ghost tours. People flock from all over to see the famous haunted doll. He's been featured on numerous television shows, has had his aura photographed, and even inspired horror movies.

Robert also receives a lot of mail, on average about three letters every day. But they aren't fan letters, most of them are letters of apology. You see many visitors to the museum fail to show Robert proper respect. Some are even openly insulting to him. Many of the letters that arrive beg for Robert's forgiveness and ask him to please lift whatever curse or negative energy he's placed upon them. Museum curator Convertitio says the museum probably has around a thousand letters, all of which are kept and cataloged in the institution's files. There's always a display of letters on the wall behind Robert's case so people can see examples of what Robert and the museum receive.

Robert also gets small gifts in the mail. At some point word got out the doll had a sweet tooth, so occasionally little boxes of chocolates or peppermints are sent to Robert. Museum staff says it does not eat any of the treats sent to Robert.

Convertitio does a once a year checkup on him, taking him out of his display case and checking every aspect of the doll for wear. She also reads his letters and email, yes, Robert gets email. She also runs his social media feeds. Robert, you see, has his own Facebook page.

Asked if she believes the doll is haunted, Convertitio responded:

*"I don't know. I really don't. I've never had a bad experience with him. I've never felt uncomfortable. It's always been a very basic relationship and I have a job to do and I go and do it. And whether there's something to it or not, he just allows me to get on with my job."*

There are frequent reports of electronic interference around Robert. Cameras, phones and other devices often freeze up or crash completely around the doll. People who dare to take Robert's picture without first asking permission usually have it the worst, experiencing ill fortune after the act.

Thomas Locklear, who worked for Key West's Ghost & Gravestones Frightseeing Tour, had his own incident with Robert. Locklear made the mistake of taking a photo of a new ghost tour guide next to Robert without first asking permission:

*"The phone I used got very hot and stopped working before I left East Martello. When I took it to Verizon the next day they said the entire inside of the phone burned up and they had never seen anything like it."* Locklear added: *"All of us who work with him (Robert) have, at the very least, seen his facial expression change. Most of us have seen him move."*

Today Robert sits on a doll-sized wooden chair in his own plexiglass case to protect him. The case however, hasn't stopped Robert from moving about. There are frequent reports from people who say they see the doll move, or change his facial expressions.

And there's another incident that has added to Robert's legend. Originally, he was alone in the display case, but now has a small, stuffed lion, nicknamed "Leo" sitting on his lap. According to a museum employee, the stuffed animal was once part of the Edna Wolkowsky dollhouse display housed in a case in the museum. One day a volunteer was cleaning the display when she noticed a pronounced space between two of the stuffed animals in the cabinet. She checked the case and found it was still locked and showed no signs of having been tampered with. She made a note to inform the museum's curator about the oddity. As she continued with her cleaning, she made her way over to Robert's display where she suddenly noticed the missing toy sitting on Robert's lap. Museum staff left it alone and it has remained with Robert ever since. It seems Robert didn't want to be in his case alone.

photo by June Nixon

## Mr. Creepy

Few would argue against the belief that ventriloquist dolls, or dummies as they are more commonly known, are the creepiest dolls out there. With a slightly menacing look in their eyes and ever-present fake smiles, you can't help but wonder what they might be thinking when they stare in your direction. The uncomfortable feeling you have around these figures is called automatonophobia - which also includes the fear of wax dummies or anything falsely representing a sentient being. This fear is completely justified if you understand the history behind it all.

Ventriloquism has a long and dark past. The art form goes back to necromancers, who would pretend to act as speakers for the dead who took up residence in the stomach of the ventriloquist. Many in the 16th century believed ventriloquism was considered witchcraft, and those who practiced this unholy magic were in league with the Devil. These practitioners were hanged or burned at the stake, so it's no wonder these disturbing dummies seemingly reflect a dark and unsettling past.

There is one particular dummy that comes to mind when investigating haunted dolls. His name is Mr. Creepy, a name given to him by his previous owner. This handmade doll sat on the bottom shelf in a vintage display case in an antique store for years, as many customers paid no attention to him or simply sneaked past him, hoping his eyes wouldn't follow. It was quite clear this doll gave folks the 'creeps,' and the previous owner felt the creepiness of his presence on a daily basis.

The story of Mr. Creepy suggests he was not meant to be alone. There was once a counterpart for him, a female dummy who we might call Mrs. Creepy. However, the owner of the store misplaced her, possibly in one of their many storage locations.

Back in the mid to late 1960s, an aged and forgotten ventriloquist artist from the vaudeville days spent his retirement years making the dolls he loved to voice from time to time. His talents would surface every so often at local events. But as the days grew longer, his hands grew weaker. Before his passing, he made two dolls in the likeness of himself and his beloved wife. Molded by his own hands, these dolls featured their once young love and their real hair as well. It seems the artist wanted these dolls to be part of them, like the children they never had.

The dolls never spent a day apart, just like the couple they were modeled after. The elderly couple came to a tragic end sometime in the late 1970s when an accident took both of their lives. After their deaths, the dolls were sold as a pair, and through the years continued to be passed around together. It was sometime in 2013 when Mr. Creepy lost sight of his better half. She was misplaced or somehow vanished in the shuffle of moving, but it seems he still pines for her

# Chapter 1: Haunted Dolls

and keeps looking around for his missing half. Not long after the loss of Mrs. Creepy, the storeowner witnessed the ever so slight turning of Mr. Creepy's head. One day he would be looking to the left, the next day to the right. Some days the owner even found Mr. Creepy's case doors sitting wide open.

When asked if he would be willing to part with Mr. Creepy, there was no hesitation from the storeowner, and Mr. Creepy was off to his new home at Spooked in Seattle to be a part of the haunted doll collection. Right away he was placed in a glass case for his protection and public viewing. One day shortly after Mr. Creepy arrived at his new home, one of Spooked in Seattle's owners heard a loud bang on glass emanating from the main area. Upon inspection, the owner found Mr. Creepy leaning his head against the glass. Surprised by the discovery, the owner quickly took a picture only to find while reviewing the image that you can see in the reflection of the glass what appears to be more of a lifelike face of a man - instead of the face of a doll.

photo by June Nixon

It seems Mr. Creepy is still looking for his companion because many of the staff members at Spooked in Seattle have witnessed him turning his head from time to time, perhaps looking for the bride he continues to miss.

Chapter 1: Haunted Dolls

# Mandy

Mandy the doll was donated to the Quesnel & District Museum in British Columbia, Canada in 1991. The doll was already over 90 years old when the museum received her. The museum's curator felt uneasy when she first took the doll. It was somewhat damaged and dirty with a frayed and faded dress. Parts of the doll's body had tears and rips, a result of age and the many children that had played with it. The truly unsettling thing was Mandy's face. The doll's forehead, just above the right eye, is cracked, causing the eye on that side to protrude slightly, making it appear to be leering back at those who look at it.

The donor wished to remain anonymous, but she told the museum she could not handle having the doll in her home anymore. Why? Because very strange things happen around Mandy.

The woman reported she would often wake up in the middle of the night to the sound of a crying child somewhere in her home. The sound would echo through the house and was so loud it couldn't be ignored. The owner would investigate, but find nothing to explain the strange crying sounds. Oddly, each time, she would find a window in her basement open, the curtains blowing in the wind, but no sign of intruders. She was convinced the crying noise was connected to the old doll, and after she donated Mandy to the museum, reported that the crying in her home stopped.

It wasn't long before curious things began to happen at the museum after Mandy's arrival. Staff members and volunteers at the Quesnel discovered their lunches disappearing out of the refrigerator, only to be found later tucked away in drawers. Other items also began to vanish: books, pictures, pencils, pens and even items that were part of museum displays. Some would reappear later, others have yet to be found.

When the doll was first received, it was put through some of the standard processes common to newly acquired items. It was taken to a work room for some basic maintenance which began with it being sealed in a plastic bag. This was done to determine if there were any insects infesting the doll. Museum staff were even more uneasy around Mandy once she was placed in the bag. Some workers said when they were in the room, they could hear the plastic bag rustling as if the doll wanted out. When they would walk over to check on Mandy, they would find her position in the bag had changed as if she had indeed been moving about. No insects were found on the doll, so none of the staff could explain either the movement or the sounds.

The next part of the museum's process involved taking a series of photographs of the doll as part of the official record. Once this was completed, Mandy was left in the lab overnight. The next morning when the staff returned to work they had quite the surprise. The room was in total disarray. Books, papers and small objects had been thrown wildly around the room and onto the floor. Larger, heavy objects had been pushed over. The lab had been completely trashed but there were no signs of a break-in and nothing was stolen. In the midst of it all, there sat Mandy where she had been left by herself overnight.

After being put on display, visitors started to complain that the doll made them feel uneasy. A statement from the museum says Mandy was first put near the entrance:

"[Mandy]...sat facing the public entranceway, visitors would stare, and talk about this doll with the cracked and broken face and sinister smile. With time, Mandy was moved to another part of the museum and carefully placed in a case by herself because rumor had it that she should not be placed with the other dolls because she would harm them."

It wasn't long before word got out about Quesnel's haunted doll and people began to visit to see what all the fuss was about. Curiosity seekers started reporting their own odd experiences with Mandy. Batteries would drain in her presence, electronic equipment would malfunction and cameras would act up. While some photos would turn out completely normal, others would be blurry as if the doll was moving when the shot was taken, or unexplained light anomalies would appear in the pictures. One woman reported the light on her video camera started turning off and on every few seconds, while she was in the room with Mandy, but once she left the camera returned to normal working condition. Countless people said they felt Mandy's eyes follow them as they moved around the room and some even claimed Mandy blinked.

Not much is known about Mandy and her origins. It's believed that the doll was made in the early 1900s, possibly in Germany. A folktale surrounding the doll claims to tell of the spirit inhabiting the antique. Allegedly the doll was found in the cellar of an old farmhouse. According to the legend, a man was walking by the place when he heard someone crying from inside. This was odd since the farmhouse had been long abandoned. The man approached the home and knocked at the door, but there was no answer. Still, the crying continued, so he entered the home thinking perhaps someone was in trouble. Once inside he realized the crying was coming from the cellar, so he went back outside and found the entrance. Making his way into the cellar, the man made a disturbing discovery. The body of a young girl, long dead, was on the floor. In her arms was the doll now known as Mandy. It's unknown how the little girl came to be in the cellar, but some believe it is her spirit that has taken up residence in the creepy little doll with the cracked face that sits in the Quesnel museum.

Chapter 1: Haunted Dolls

# Letta the Gypsy Doll

In 1972 in Australia, Kerry Walton returned to his birthplace for his grandmother's funeral. While in the small village, Kerry would confront a childhood fear of an old house nearby many believed to be haunted. For decades local children avoided this long abandoned structure for fear the ghosts would get them. Kerry, however, had grown more curious of the creaky old house and ventured into the darkness with a flashlight in hand.

Kerry collected vintage bottles, and hoped the old place might yield some for his collection. He searched in all the nooks and darkened corners for hidden treasures. It wasn't until he ventured under the house, through the cobwebs and dirt, that he caught sight of a disturbing face staring back at him. Startled, he jerked back almost knocking himself out as he hit his head on a floor beam above him. He believed he had discovered a dead child, but was surprised to discover it was nothing more than a decomposing doll.

Nevertheless drawn to the doll, Kerry crept closer as the doll locked him in with its unsettling stare. Its clothes crumbled to nothing when Kerry reached out and pulled the wooden doll closer to him. He was curious to find out how this doll came to rest under the house and survive this long under harsh conditions. While inspecting the doll, he discovered it had real human hair, but the real oddity was the scalp could be removed to reveal a brain inside. Compelled to take it, Kerry returned home with the odd naked marionette, a souvenir he would soon learn would become extremely hard to part with.

After his grandmothers funeral, Kerry and his brother set off on their long journey home, unaware the supernatural power of the doll was about to unfold. Kerry placed the ratty doll in a bag and shoved it in the back of the van. Meanwhile his brother took to driving while he rested in the passenger seat. Fast asleep, Kerry woke to his brother nudging him; his brother had heard strange sounds coming from the back of the van. It sounded like rustling around in a bag, as if the doll was moving around on its own, and this was freaking him out. To put his brother at ease, Kerry took over driving the rest of the way, only to hear the same sounds from behind him.

After a nerve-racking long drive home, Kerry finally summoned the courage to open the bag and see what was going on. Nothing seemed out of the ordinary, but when he introduced the creepy dolly to his dog, the animal became vicious, growling and barking hysterically at the doll.

A month later, Kerry learned the old house which had stood for well over two hundred years was finally torn down. If it hadn't been for Kerry, the doll would have perished, and he believes the doll may have called on him for its rescue.

The doll immediately made those who looked at it uneasy, and his family complained that the doll seemed to always be looking at them with its cold dark eyes. His children were known to play with the doll during the day, but at night they could be heard screaming in fright as the doll sat calmly watching them. Kerry eventually decided to store the doll under his house, but on rare occasions they would wake in the middle of the night, hearing the doll scream "Letta me out! Letta me out!" Fear caused the family to keep Letta at a safe distance beneath the family home for nearly five years. Later, Kerry wanted to sell his house and needed more money for their new home. Curious to see if the vintage doll might have some value, he decided to take the doll to a museum in Sydney. Oddly, once in the car it began to downpour on what was supposed to be a clear day.

The folks at the Sydney museum discovered the doll was somewhere between 170 to 200 years old due to the nails in his shoes. They also believed it was the work of a Romanian gypsy craftsman. The gypsies of that era used effigy's for what they called Spirit Transference, where the soul of loved ones would possess dolls as homes for the recently departed.

Now fueled with some history of Letta's age and the rarity of the doll, he immediately listed the doll in hopes to get a generous sum. In no time an offer was agreed upon, but Letta's power of persuasion was about to surface once again. Kerry went to load the doll in the car when another heavy rain started up - a common phenomenon that seemed to happen whenever Letta was taken out in public. Once he arrived at the buyer's house Kerry found himself unable to get out of his car. For some strange reason he just couldn't move. Glued to his seat Kerry sat for what seemed like hours, frozen from the chills going up and down his back. It wasn't until he made the decision to keep the doll that he was once again able to move, and he drove away without completing the sale.

Letta's story became known and the doll became a bit of a celebrity featured on many talk shows. A host of a daytime program arranged for a meeting between Letta and a highly regarded psychic. The doll arrived on a rainy day at the psychic's office only to have a painting fall off the wall and the clock stop. Letta was placed on the psychic's lap, and as the crew filmed their interaction, the doll's head slowly started to turn on its own. Everyone standing around saw this and heard the sounds of the wooden neck creaking. One cameraman turned completely white and ran out the door.

The psychic herself felt the presence of a child trapped inside the doll. The spirit was six years old and had drowned during a storm in Romania. It was his grieving father that had fashioned the doll and had his child's soul transferred into the wooden vessel. The psychic believed the child to be frightened and confused throughout the centuries, and further claimed it was an Australian immigrant responsible for bringing the doll to Kerry's village and storing it under the house.

During the filming of another show, with more than 200 viewers on a rainy day, a crowd quietly gathered around the doll only to hear a woman screaming as Letta's head again started to turn of its own accord.

While doing a show at a local grocery store, the shoppers were shaken when a woman, not even in the audience, but from the back of the store started screaming "there's an evil presence here!," and then passed out. Letta has been known to cause sudden terror to those who look upon him or even those who are close by.

Today the doll still remains in Kerry's family's custody. Nothing evil has ever been experienced - in fact, just the opposite. It seems Letta brings more good luck than bad. From time to time you may find the doll has moved. Dogs still don't like him. It rains whenever he ventures out, or his expression may appear to change from happy to sad.

Most recently Kerry's granddaughter posted online about witnessing strange events around the doll, from his eyes changing color, to him wiggling around while sitting on her lap. She goes on to say that, "We don't like to think of it as we are stuck with him, he is a family member."

# The Haunted Raggedy Ann

## "Warning, Positively Do Not Open"

So says the sign on a Raggedy Ann doll sitting in a specially made case in a museum in Connecticut. The doll known as Annabelle became internationally known after it served as the inspiration for cinematic depictions in "The Conjuring" and "Annabelle." A sequel, "Annabelle 2" is scheduled for an upcoming release. The doll depicted in the films looks very different from the real Annabelle, but the creepy stories are based on true events.

Annabelle's real story begins in 1970 when a mother purchases an antique Raggedy Ann doll from a second-hand store. The doll was supposed to be a birthday present for her daughter Donna. Donna was a college student about to graduate with a degree in nursing. She resided in a small apartment with a roommate, another nurse named Angie. Donna loved the doll and put it on her bed as a decorative item. Before long, strange things began to happen. The doll would move on its own. The movements were relatively unnoticeable at first, but the doll's position would change. The more the women payed attention to the doll, the more noticeable Annabelle's movements became.

The movements became even more dramatic. Donna and Angie would come home and find the doll in a completely different room from the one in which they had left it. Sometimes, the doll would be found sitting on the couch with its legs crossed and its arms folded, as if it was angry. Other times the doll would be standing, leaning against a chair in the dining room. On several occasions, Donna placed the doll on the couch, and when she returned she would find the doll back in her bedroom, with the door closed.

Annabelle's movements weren't the only disturbing things about the doll. About a month into the women's experiences with the doll, they began to find messages written in pencil on parchment paper. The handwriting looked like it belonged to a small child, and the statements would say things like "Help Us." Even more disturbing was the girl's didn't keep parchment paper in their apartment. Was Annabelle manifesting the notes out of thin air? No one knew where the paper with the strange messages originated from.

One night Donna came home and again found the doll sitting on her bed. This time something was different. Upon inspecting the doll

Donna found what appeared to be drops of blood on the back of its hands and chest. The women were scared and decided it was time to call in some experts.

They contacted a medium and a séance was held in an attempt to find some answers. The psychic told Donna and Angie the doll was inhabited by the spirit of a dead girl named "Annabelle Higgins." The psychic also said the Higgins girl had resided on the property before the apartments were built on the site. When the little girl was only seven years old, her lifeless body was found in the field where the building now stands. The little girl's spirit told the medium she was comfortable with the nurses and wanted to stay with them. The women felt sorry for the girl's spirit, so they gave her permission to remain with them and the doll.

That turned out to be a big mistake.

Whatever was inhabiting the Raggedy Ann was certainly not an innocent child. Soon, things took an even darker turn. A friend of Donna's, a man named Lou, suffered a strange attack by the spirit in the doll and received a series of burning claw marks on his chest. Donna began to realize things associated with the doll were much more serious than first thought, so she contacted a priest at the Episcopal church, who in turn contacted Ed and Lorraine Warren.

The Warrens quickly determined a demonic entity had taken up residence in the doll. After Donna's house was cleansed and blessed, the Warrens took Annabelle away. The drive was perilous. At each curve the car swerved and stalled, the power steering and brakes kept failing - and all the while the possessed doll just sat alone in the back seat. Calling on a higher power, Ed Warren doused the doll with holy water, and the car finally returned to its normal functionality, the couple making it home safely.

Once they had the doll back at their home, the Warrens noticed it was still quite disturbed. The doll would levitate and vanish from one spot, only to reappear elsewhere. A special case was built for the doll where it still resides today. Over the years many people have had negative experiences connected to Annabelle, and the popularity of the recent films has made her one of the most well-known haunted dolls in the world.

Chapter 1: Haunted Dolls

## Joliet's Curse

It's not uncommon to have family heirlooms passed from generation to generation. Most tend to be items like a great-great-grandmother's wedding ring, or maybe some antique furniture, or perhaps for some, an old doll. But what happens if that doll is cursed?

A great tragedy followed one family for more than a century, and affected four generations of women in its throes. The supposed curse prevented the family's women from giving birth to a male heir. Each woman suffered the same ordeal: giving birth to two children, a son and a daughter. But whenever one of the women gave birth to a healthy boy, the newborn son was lost to a sudden and mysterious illness, on the third day of his young life. A tragedy spawned again, and again, and yet again.

This haunting curse was traced to a doll that was given to a great-grandmother, who received the doll as a present from a family friend during her pregnancy with her second child. What was unknown at the time was the friend who gave her the doll had become jealous of the fact that she herself was unable to bear children, and may have had feelings for the great-grandmother's husband as well. The doll, given out of this resentment, became cursed, as tragedy struck the family time and time again.

In August of 1945 the haunting of the doll became more apparent after another one of the women within the lineage had a son that died. The great-grandmother of the hierarchy would perpetually awaken to the sounds of her departed son's and grandson's crying and screaming - from all of the generations of lost boys. She found those sounds seemed to come from the doll named Joliet - and from nowhere else, in spite of the supposed curse. On another occasion she even heard the doll giggle as their cat rubbed up against it. The doll became a constant reminder of repeated loss, as the eerie cries brought back memories of her son and those before. But knowing their son was connected to Joliet offered comfort as well. If her son was in Joliet, she could protect him and offer some sort of care.

Throughout the years, Joliet's curse would strike again and again, eliminating the newborn sons, and each of the mothers realized the spirits of their absent boys were attached to the doll named Joliet. Each mother cared for the doll just like they would for their own sons, had they lived.

Joliet holds tight to the four souls she collected, and waits for more, as the haunted doll is passed from mother to daughter to protect the lost children. Even creepier, the cries of the four babies are only heard by the women who suffered the tragic losses. The present owner of the doll, Anna, the most recent member of the family suffering Joliet's curse, says the hardest part is wondering if her daughter will experience the same things her mother, grandmother and great-grandmother have all experienced.

## Okiku the Living Doll

Japan, 1918. Seventeen year old Eikichi Suzuki is visiting Sapporo on the island of Hokkaido for a marine exhibition. Walking along Tanuki-koji, Sapporo's famous shopping street, Eikichi decides to purchase a special doll for his two year old sister, Okiku. The doll is about sixteen inches tall and dressed in a traditional Japanese kimono. The life-like porcelain white face is set with black beads for eyes, and the doll's coal black hair is cut at shoulder length.

When Eikichi presented the doll to Okiku, she was overjoyed with the gift. She kept the doll with her constantly and even named it after herself, Okiku. For a year, the little girl and her special doll were constant companions, then a terrible tragedy befell young Okiku. She contracted influenza and the complications lead to her death. The devastated family went into mourning and placed their daughter's beloved doll on the family altar, the location where they said their daily prayers, including prayers to their deceased child. Soon they began to notice something strange. The doll Okiku was changing. Its hair which had been at shoulder length was getting longer. While the hair had been straight and even when it was in their daughter's possession, now the hair became uneven with some strands growing longer than others. It wasn't long before the doll's hair had grown all the way down to its knees. The family tried trimming the hair, but it soon grew back, again, all the way to the knees. They fully believed their daughter's spirit was restless and had taken up residency in the porcelain doll.

In 1938 the family decided to relocate to Sakhalin. Preparing for the move, they were afraid to move the doll to their new home but also unwilling to dispose of it. They took the doll to the Mannenji Temple in Iwamizawa, Hokkaido, Japan. Meeting with the temple's priest, the family explained the strange qualities of the doll and their belief that their daughter's spirit was trapped within. The temple accepted the doll into their care where it remains to this day. The temple's priest have long observed the regular growth of Okiku's hair and trimming it has become a regular duty at the temple.

Around the temple there are various photos showing Okiku with varying lengths of hair. The doll rests quietly in a simple wooden box. No matter how often its hair is trimmed, it continues to grow back. The haunted Okiku doll has become well known in Japan where it has found its way into popular culture, including films and novels. To date no one has been able to explain why the Okiku's hair continues to grow. Samples of the hair have been analyzed and verified to be human hair. Okiku remains at the Mannenji temple, still dressed in a traditional kimono, coal black eyes gazing out at visitors, and her hair still grows.

Chapter 1: Haunted Dolls

## Pupa

The name Pupa means "Doll" in Italian. Created in the 1920s, this lovely doll stood 14 inches tall. She had a felt head, arms and legs and was made in the likeness of her owner – a child born in Trieste, Italy. More than made in her human's likeness, Pupa's coif was made from the little girl's hair.

From the very beginning, the child formed a strong bond with her precious doll. The two were inseparable. With her owner, Pupa travelled quite extensively throughout Europe and the United States. Doll and child even wore the same outfits. When the child's grandmother passed away sometime near the end of the second World War, the little girl had one of her grandmother's buttons sewn onto Pupa's blue dress as a keepsake.

The child's family often noted Pupa appeared alive in the many pictures of the two, but no one seemed too concerned – even when the little girl claimed her doll was 'alive' with a will of its own. The two seemed to talk often throughout the years. The growing child had the perfect friend to tell her secrets too. To whom would Pupa reveal them?

Throughout the years as the little girl grew into an adult, the doll continued to be a dear and close friend. Pupa's little girl eventually became a woman and moved from Trieste to America, where she died in 2005. Before her passing she shared her Pupa stories with her grandchildren, including one incredible tale in which Pupa saved her life.

After her passing the family decided to preserve the doll. Dressed in her original blue suit with a large blue bow in her hair, she was placed inside a glass case in honor of their beloved mother and grandmother. That's when Pupa made herself known. It seems Pupa doesn't like being confined in such a small environment. Shortly after placing the doll in the case, a member of the family saw smudges on the glass and decided to clean it. After exhaling hot air onto the glass, an image came into view – what appeared to be child's fingertips pressed into the glass with the words "Pupa hate" written beside them.

To date Pupa periodically changes positions, and her facial features appear to change expression. Some say she manages to get out only to be found sitting outside the glass case. Pupa is also known to move things away from her if she doesn't like them. And if she wants your attention, she'll knock on the glass. One member of the family witnessed Pupa moving around and grabbed a camera to film the doll's abilities. However, when Pupa stopped and the family sat to review the footage, all they found was a fog-like substance and the words "Pupa no." Today the owners keep their family history and the doll's location a secret, both to protect themselves and Pupa.

Chapter 1: Haunted Dolls

# Peggy

Imagine a doll so haunted, that simply viewing photos or videos of it online can lead to nausea, crippling headaches, chest pains and even heart attacks.

Meet Peggy.

Now owned by UK-based paranormal investigator Jayne Harris, Peggy has been wreaking havoc online via photographs and videos posted by Harris in her Facebook group, Haunted Dolls.

Harris, based in Shrewsbury, Shropshire, received the doll from its previous owner who reported a series of frightening incidents. The woman would wake up hot and shaken after terrible nightmares. No matter where she moved the doll in her home, the horrible dreams continued. The woman called in a local priest to bless the home, but after two separate visits, there was no improvement, and things actually got worse. Not only did the night terrors continue, but the woman became very ill with a high fever and started to suffer hallucinations. Fortunately she recovered, but enough was enough. She googled "haunted dolls" looking for a way to deal with Peggy and found Harris's group. She sent the doll to Harris and said she wanted nothing more to do with the possessed figure.

Harris began to post pictures of Peggy online, and right away it was clear the doll's ill effects had an extensive reach. Reports began to flow into her inbox. Countless people described strange phenomena as a result of viewing photos of Peggy the doll. One woman claimed her computer froze on a picture of Peggy and the room turned ice cold. According to Harris:

*"She then said she felt someone in the room with her and could hear them moving around. This lady was messaging me at the time via Facebook, asking me to quickly advise her on what to do. I took Peggy down into an isolation area and requested that she cease her tormenting. Apparently everything returned to normal."*

Another woman reported that light bulbs in her home started blowing when she began to speak about Peggy. Other reports were of overwhelming anxiety and strange visions of mental institutions and abuse. But the consequences of Peggy's online presence didn't end there. When Harris posted a video of the haunted doll, a wide range of reports rolled in from people who were suffering terribly after viewing it. Reports included those experiencing nausea, crippling headaches and chest pains. According to Harris, one viewer, a British woman, even claimed her heart attack was a result of seeing the haunted Peggy video. Harris says that around 80% of the people who have any kind of contact with Peggy, including online, experience some kind of negative reaction.

Jayne Harris has had her own negative experiences that she believes are connected to the creepy doll. She's had migraines and felt completely drained after working with Peggy. She says she has never worked on a case so intense.

*"Just the other night we held a session with her and I made lots of notes as the pendulum was going crazy. The next morning, I couldn't find my notepad anywhere, and when I did find it, I couldn't even reach it. It had been placed up in the joists of the ceiling in our basement. My husband had to use a ladder to get it. Many people who saw the picture felt that she did not want me to tell people the information I had gained."*

Little is known about the history of the doll, so Harris and her team have been busy utilizing various psychic techniques in an attempt to learn more. She says Peggy had an aversion to a crucifix placed around her neck. Two mediums have stated they believe the spirit inhabiting Peggy is Jewish and has a link to the holocaust. Curiously, automatic writing sessions done in Peggy's presence have brought forth the word "star" as well as the name "David," possibly implying a link to the Jewish Star of David.

Others believe the spirit is that of a woman born in London in 1946 who later died of a chest related condition, possibly asthma. Another curious connection when considering many people report chest pains after viewing Peggy. Whatever the history of the spirit, each medium who has read the doll picks up that the entity is restless, frustrated and suffered much persecution in life.

There are also stories that claim Peggy shows up in people's dreams. One woman reported to Harris that Peggy had appeared to her in a dream, issuing a warning about one of the woman's cats. The next morning, she awoke to find her cat very ill. The animal died the next day.

One medium known as Lindy had a unique set of experiences she connected to Peggy and posted her impressions about the doll online:

*"When I commented my thoughts and feelings, all my comments were duplicated—no one else's, just mine. I tried commenting on other threads and nothing happened, but as soon as I went back to that one, the same thing happened. My dog started barking and my face became very hot and flushed. I felt like I wasn't alone. I ended up apologizing to Peggy as I felt maybe she disproved of us chatting about her and my symptoms stopped."*

Lindy's connection with Peggy had some positive consequences, too. After watching a video about Peggy, something pushed Lindy to have a long overdue conversation with her daughter about the girl's mental health issues.

*"My daughter has been unwell for months and things were strained and stressful. Late that morning, I found myself having a much needed heart-to-heart with her. All the things I had wanted to say for months were just flowing from my mouth. I've found it very difficult communicating in such a way with her due to her illness. I felt that Peggy had helped me."*

Lindy had no idea that an automatic writing session with Peggy was taking place at the same time as her conversation with her daughter. When she went online, she saw images of the session and the messages received. Among them was one that seemed to be directed specifically at her:

*"The words 'Lindy girl explanation draw a line' were written on the paper. I couldn't believe my eyes. It was basically what had just been talked about between me and my daughter."*

Harris says that people continue to contact her to report being tormented after viewing Peggy. Each time Harris takes the doll into an isolation area and simply asks her to stop. The tactic usually does the trick. Numerous psychics have offered to clear the doll of its negative attachment, or to take the Peggy doll themselves, but Harris isn't interested. Instead she prefers to keep the haunted doll herself and continue various experiments to study the chaos Peggy creates.

*"In order to do the work I do well, I have to approach each case as a skeptic initially and look for 'normal' explanations for things. If it were one or two occasions that things were happening on, I could do that, but with Peggy I just know there's something more."*

The notorious video clip remains online for those brave enough to view it. It's posted with the warning to "watch at your own risk."

# Haunted Harold

Haunted objects are hard to come by, unless you do a search on eBay. Today you can pretty much find anything your heart desires, from a grilled cheese sandwich with the image of the Virgin Mary to William Shatner's kidney stone.

It was in 2004 when the first haunted doll made its eBay premier, with this story by the seller Greg Mishka:

*I had arrived at the flea market fairly late in the day, when most people were packing up to go home. That is when I saw an elderly man placing the doll in a box. It looked interesting, so I asked the man if I could see it... the conversation went something like this.*

Man: you don't want to see this doll

Me: sure I do, what do you want for it?

Man: well, that's a good question, because it's very old... (the man looked like he was going to begin to cry) ... it was my son's, I bought it for him when he was born, and he passed away a few years after...this doll has sat in my work shed for over 60 years. I wasn't going to bring it out today, but I figured I just needed to get it out of there...anyways, I want 20 bucks for it. I gave the guy 20 bucks, put it in a bag, and walked away. When I was half way down the aisle, the man came running over, visibly out of breath...

Man: I have to warn you about something, I can't just let you take him like this...the reason it has been in my shed, is that the doll brought an eerie presence into our house after our son died...we would hear crying and singing from his bedroom...when we went to check it out, there was nothing, just the doll.. other things started to happen, and the priest told me I should burn the doll, I tried and tried, but it would barely burn, that's why his arms and head and legs are so worn.. anyways I just wanted to let you know...

I told him ok, and chuckled to myself as I walked away... that was until I got home, and my life has never been the same... Two days later my cat died, my girlfriend left me for the pool guy, I began to have chronic migraines, and this is only 2 days after purchasing the doll! A week later I began to hear children laughing and crying in my basement.

Every time I would go to check it out, of course, nothing...

*This doll has been in an armadillo coffin in my basement for the last year and half, and I need to get rid of it... I really do believe it's cursed, sometimes I touch it, and it seems like it has a pulse, maybe I'm just paranoid, maybe not... The cursed doll measures 21" tall.*

*His/her/its head, arms, and legs are all composition. The eyes are closed when it's lying down. Please ask any and all questions before you bid on this doll. I have not had it out of the coffin for years, so if anything else happens this week I will be sure to let you know.*

Haunted Harold became a huge sensation with an ending bid of close to $700. However, the winner wasn't able to pay up and Harold was back on the market.

In 2009, Greg published an article on the web telling the true story of Haunted Harold. It seems Harold wasn't so haunted; it was just a gimmick to help sell the doll. In fact, after the popularity of Haunted Harold's bidding war, many others jumped on the bandwagon as the production of haunted dolls became a huge moneymaker. I'm sure you can guess how it all ended. Yes, a majority of these "possessed" dolls were indeed faked.

Kathy, a family friend from Ireland, offered $300 for the creepy old doll in hopes of reselling it for a profit. Yet, while in her care, she began experiencing unlucky events within a short amount of time.

After a friend of hers saw the doll back on eBay, she wanted to see it for herself by paying the doll a special visit. It was a month after that personal encounter that her friend was diagnosed with a brain tumor, which eventually took her life.

A short time after that tragedy, another friend inquired about Harold during a dinner party. So she gave him an introduction. A month later that friend died from falling down a flight of stairs.

Anthony Quinata took responsibility for Harold after buying him from Kathy. Today he claims Harold's haunting abilities continue to torment the current owner. Anthony has since published a book and website devoted to the strange encounters he's experienced while Harold's been in his care. It had gotten so bad he locked the doll up for a short time, only to find things aren't so bad if the doll is out and about.

Harold presents so many questions. Is Haunted Harold real?

Has all the attention the public and his owner give him the power to really become a cursed doll? Maybe Haunted Harold really is... HAUNTED.

Chapter 1: Haunted Dolls

# The Devil Baby Doll

The mystical city of New Orleans overflows with legends. From Voodoo Queens and "Rootworkers," to pirate ghosts and vampires, the city is full of magic and spirits. But lurking in the shadows of the back streets and alleys is a particularly creepy legend known as the devil baby doll.

Sometimes called the "Devil Baby of Bourbon Street," the little monster was adopted by the Voodoo Queen Marie LaVeau, and even christened by the notorious Madame LaLaurie.

The story begins in the 1800s when a young woman from one of the city's powerful families married a wealthy Scotsman. Heading into the beneficial marriage, the woman left an angry lover behind and he did not take the matter lightly. The scorned man sought out Marie LaVeau, the Voodoo Queen of New Orleans and paid her to work her mojo on the new bride so that he could have his revenge. LaVeau laid a curse on the woman. When the woman later went into labor with the Scotsman's offspring, she died at childbirth but not before bringing forth a misshapen baby said to be the progeny of the devil himself.

The baby was scorned by those who saw it for they feared it would bring darkness into their lives, so the Voodoo Queen herself took the child in and cared for it. The baby was christened by the infamous Madame LaLaurie and it lived to plague the city's French Quarter for many years. Legend says when the baby passed, it was buried alongside Marie LaVeau in her vault in Saint Louis Cemetery Number 1.

Other stories claim the baby lived on in a ghostly form, a child-sized devil lurking in the darkness. Citizens of the Big Easy spoke in whispered tones about the devil baby. They feared it and believed it hid in the shadows of the back streets and alleys, waiting to cause misfortune to any who crossed its path.

As a means of protection, they began to carve images of the devil baby out of gourds. They believed by hanging the images outside of their homes, they could prevent the real devil baby from intruding into their houses and cursing their lives.

Soon, "Rootworkers" or magical practitioners of Hoodoo, started using the little devil dolls to curse people. The carved babies would show up on the doorstep of the unfortunate target of someone's ire.

It was a frightening item for one to find at their door.

Fear of the devil baby grew around the city. These carved dolls were primitive but were made to more closely resemble the real devil baby than were the carved gourds previously used. The dolls would be dressed in children's clothing and made to stand on their own with a stuffed body and arms that could be moved. The face of the dolls was always the same, with leering, glassy eyes and little devil horns that protruded from the forehead. A knotted, jute tail would complete the devilish appearance. At some point, a woman who had seen the real devil baby as a child confirmed the similarity between the dolls and the real child.

It's reported that Marie LaVeau didn't approve of the use of devil baby images and laid a curse on all the dolls. A curse many believe is still active.

In fact, the notorious devil baby is still creating waves of fear and curiosity on the streets of New Orleans. In modern times, newer versions of the dolls have begun to appear around the city. It's said they are exact replicas of the original dolls used by Hoodoo practitioners and because of this, they are believed to be possessed.

Most of the old, original devil baby dolls are long gone, or sitting in family heirloom cabinets or private curio collections. On the rare occasion one has shown up on the market, the prices are usually extremely high.

Enter New Orleans artist Ricardo Pustanio who claims to own remnants of one of the original devil baby dolls from the 1900s. Based on the artifact in his possession, Pustanio began creating his own devil baby dolls. Customers who purchased these highly sought after pieces say Pustanio's dolls are also haunted.

When he made his first set of devil dolls, Pustanio said that when they were gathered together, whispering and rustling sounds could be heard. Thinking he should separate the dolls, the artist convinced several of his friends to each take a doll for safe keeping. Almost right away, Pustanio's friends all wanted to return the dolls to him, reporting strange occurrences in their homes after taking the dolls.

One person reported the devil baby moved on its own when no one was around. Left in a closet in the man's spare bedroom, he would come home to find the closet door open and the doll laying out on the carpet.

## Chapter 1: Haunted Dolls

Another couple reported the doll they were keeping overturned items and threw beads from a bead-making kit around the room. No one else was in the home when the incident occurred.

There have been so many reports of the dolls moving on their own and causing turmoil in the homes of those who take them, that Pustanio now sells the dolls with a "Buyer Beware" warning.

Although they remain highly sought after, some people who purchased one of the devil babies quickly decided to sell it, disturbed at the presence that seems to follow the little dolls.

Paranormal investigator Sylvia Cross bought one of the devil babies to add to her collection of creepy dolls. Even she was disturbed by the amount of activity the thing exhibited. She reported weird shuffling sounds and the cries of a baby coming from the doll. Her cats refuse to go near the doll and won't even enter the room where it sits.

"Some objects are just 'born' for lack of a better word, with a dark soul. I think the Devil Baby is one of those objects. If you look into its eyes you can almost discern the flicker of a trapped, unhappy soul."

A disturbed, trapped soul? A dark curse from the Voodoo Queen herself? Decide for yourself. If you're brave enough, Pustanio's dolls are available. They're all one of a kind and can even be made to order, but remember, purchase at your own risk, you may be taking home a piece of the spirit of one of New Orleans' creepiest legends.

# Chapter 2: Strange & Curious Toys

## Jack is in the box

*All around the mulberry bush,*

*The monkey chased the weasel.*

*The monkey stopped to pull up his sock,*

*Pop! goes the weasel.*

You may not know the lyrics to this old-fashioned children's song, but its melody will haunt you with its tinny chime seeping out as you slowly turn the crank of the box, cautiously waiting for Jack to pop out and greet you.

Folklore tells an unsettling tale about the Jack in the box. It is believed the startling toy originates from the 14th century, created by an Englishman known as Sir John Schorne. History depicts in many portraits him holding a boot with a devil inside it. The story goes that Sir John saved the troubled village of North Marston in Buckinghamshire by casting the devil into a boot. Which could be why the French refer to the Jack-in-the-box as *'diable en boît'* meaning 'boxed devil.' The toy itself came about 500 years later after Sir John's death in 1313.

The Jack in the box is a toy that is either loved or hated by children throughout the centuries. In fact most can identify their fear when confronted by the box with a crank. What is lurking inside? For one vintage toy collector that question offered more than she expected.

Her encounter started by seeking out the toys she was most fond of as a child. Dolls, tea sets and many other childish things began to fill her room as her collection grew through the years.

It was on one of her antique outings that she came across a Bozo the clown jack in the box looking down on her with its worn crooked smile. Being a big fan of Bozo she knew she had to have it. She pulled the toy down from the shelf and preceded to test it just to make sure it was working correctly. All was well.

Once home she cleared a space on her shelf for her new toy. However, due to the wear and tear the clown seemed to carry an almost sinister look that began to unsettle the toy owner. She decided to push the clown back into his box, firmly closing the lid shut. It was that night when the toy made its intentions known.

In her dream, she felt the clown holding her down as he chanted over and over *"I stand around a one-foot high; Don't fool with me or you might die; Where I come from, no one knows; But wherever I go, more fear grows; Treat me well and you will see; What old Jack can do for thee."*

The next morning she was surprised to see good old Bozo peering out of his box as if to warn her once more. Not wanting to believe in the foolishness of ghosts, she ignored the signs and proceeded to push the clown back down into the box and go on with her day. Things went on with no other signs of trouble, until a few days later when she was awoken by what she claimed was the chiming of the jack in the box. However, once she was fully awake there was clearly no sound, but Bozo had again escaped from the box and stared down at her.

"This is just a silly toy!" she kept repeating to herself. Once again she pulled the toy down from the shelf, pushed Bozo back inside and continued to test it by turning the crank. The old music box played and played the same tune over and over. But this time the clown refused to jump out. She tapped the lid, again and again, but still nothing. She even repeatedly slammed the box on the table. Nevertheless, the clown remained inside. "Good! Stay there!" she then shoved the box on the shelf and went back to sleep.

However, the next morning the creepy clown was back, offering her that same crooked smile. She had had enough. She tossed the box into the trash and the clown was never seen again.

Chapter 2: Strange & Curious Toys

# The Murderous Puppet

*"...without warning my throat suddenly went really tight. I've never had anyone's hands around my throat before so it was really scary. While I was choking, I tried to wake my wife, but it took her ages to come round. When she did, I remember looking straight at the puppet sitting on the drawers near our bed and realizing it was him."*

The creepy account is from John, the original owner of a murderous puppet that was in his possession for several months.

The puppet is in the likeness of an old man and was made in the 1960s. Its face is intricately carved and it has the traditional cross bars and strings attached to manipulate its movements. John inherited the puppet after his father's death. He was never comfortable with it but kept it because it had been one of his father's favorite belongings.

"My first memory of it was when I was 19, it used to hang in my Dad's spare room. I never liked it and people would never sleep in the same room as the puppet because there was a weird atmosphere in the room."

Shortly after he inherited the toy, John and his wife began to experience minor paranormal activity around their home.

"Two weeks after inheriting the puppet I started to have really bad headaches and feeling dizzy, which I never thought could be the puppet. I struggled to sleep because I'd have nightmares where an old man would hold me down or would be sitting at the edge of my bed.

I cleared out all of my dad's belongings apart from the puppet, which I left on the drawer by my bed for some reason, and that night it felt like I was being chocked. I was wide awake in bed and thought I saw a shadow move from one side of the window to the other and worried something was trying to scare us."

John contacted Jayne Harris, a paranormal investigator specializing in haunted objects. When Harris investigated John's house, she discovered wild readings on the puppet, confirming there was something unusual about the toy. John promptly gave Harris the item. He reported that both he and his wife felt much better as soon as the puppet was out of their house and their lives.

Harris placed the puppet in a sealed, glass container blessed with holy water. She and her team aimed night vision cameras at the case and proceeded to film the toy for three months. The team caught what they believe to be some amazing footage: the puppet moving on its own.

In the dead of night, the cameras caught the wooden toy's operating cross slowly moving upright and then crashing down into one of the glass sides of the sealed case. Harris says the footage left her dumbstruck:

"I've never had anything as exciting as this. I've caught pictures of mists, orbs, and shadows, but nothing as physical as this video evidence. Normally, you expect to see an orb or shadow, but as soon as I saw a bit of movement and a glint from the metal hooks, it made me jump and I knew we'd recorded something important."

Harris says that prior to the footage, there were some anomalous sounds such as bumps and knocking around the puppet, but nothing definitive until the video.

"Now we're going to keep filming with motion sensors as this is just one video and we want to build a bigger picture."

Harris, who also owns the haunted Peggy doll, sometimes employs psychic mediums to gather information on the objects she collects. A medium who read the puppet informed Harris the object has the spirit of an old man attached to it. The medium claims the old man's spirit is mocking the team by demonstrating he can move the puppet as he pleases, despite it being locked in a sealed container.

"Our ultimate goal is to find out as much as we can about the spirit and then try to understand why he is still here. The container is only a physical thing, so in theory something that's not of the physical world can pass in and out."

The case is completely secure to keep the experiments as controlled as possible. There are no doors on the cabinet and getting inside it requires lifting it off its base. When Harris informed the puppet's former owner John about the footage, he wasn't surprised:

"The fact that there's video evidence now makes me uncomfortable to be honest, I wouldn't watch it as I don't need any more proof that it was haunted. I lived with the puppet for months and it did more than enough to convince me."

Chapter 2: Strange & Curious Toys

## Suicide Mickey

When it comes to Disney cartoons, we think the "Once Upon a Time" tales are uplifting stories of adventure and romance, or possibly even about the magic that a wish upon a star could grant. But according to urban legend, there is said to be a lost vintage cartoon from the 1930's known as "Suicide Mickey" or "Mickey in Hell." It's purported to be a continuous loop of a black-and-white cartoon featuring a depressed-looking Mickey walking across a city landscape accompanied by eerie piano music as it fades to black.

Nothing unusual was even thought about it when the rumor was revealed, in fact Walt Disney himself found humor in comical, failed attempts of someone ending their own life. In October of 1930 a comic strip was produced by Disney and cartoonist Floyd Gottfredson, where Mickey realizes Minnie is having an affair, and he proceeds to try to take his own life by first shooting himself, then jumping from a bridge, and lastly, exposing himself to a gas leak. All these failed endeavors ended in some comical way, but Mickey's last attempt at suicide would be a hit too close to home for Walt himself.

It was in 1937 when Walt and his brother Roy made it big with their feature film, Snow White and the Seven Dwarfs, which grossed over $3 million with its first release. This success allowed the brothers to purchase a home for their parents. Their mother Flora complained that the furnace in their new home wasn't working properly, so Walt sent a couple of studio repairmen to the house to fix the problem. It seems these men didn't do their job correctly, and on November 6, 1938, Flora died of asphyxiation from the furnace fumes. This tragic event put Walt into a very depressed state. Many believe it was around this time the "Suicide Mickey" was produced by Walt himself, only to be forgotten about.

For decades it must have sat in the Disney vault until the publication of Mickey classics was to be released on DVD. It is believed that Leonard Maltin (no relation to the well known film critic) was reviewing the vintage cartoons for the series and had transferred the unsuspecting short to his computer. Noticing the cartoon was actually over nine minutes long and not the reported few minutes, he decided to investigate the rest of the footage.

The sequence began with the saddened Mickey walking along while the creepy piano music played before fading into darkness. Silence filled the room as Maltin waited patiently for something to happen. It was around the sixth minute of the footage when things took an unnerving turn. The cartoon blared back to life with sounds of crying, yelling and gurgling which grew louder and louder. Buildings in the background began to stretch back and forth in all directions as the video became warped and distorted. While all this was happening Mickey revealed a rather sinister smile.

By the seventh minute, the background sounds turned into terrifying screams and the cartoon became more and more distorted as Mickey's face began to fall apart. His face contorted, revealing something more demonic than the iconic mouse, and his eyeballs fell out and down to his chin, while the buildings in the backdrop broke apart and floated in midair.

Maltin had enough and couldn't bear another minute of the torturous scene and sent for another employee to finish watching the last few minutes. All he asked was that they keep notes of the remainder of the macabre cartoon. As Maltin's relief watched the remainder of the short, the screaming got louder as the distorted video played on until shortly after the eighth minute. It seems the video abruptly stopped, the normal Mickey face we all know appearing as the credits slowing wound by accompanied by a broken music box playing in the background. The employee stumbled out of the viewing room, pale, feverish and panicky. He muttered under his breath seven times "Real suffering is not known." A security guard on his rounds walked by only to have the distraught employee grab the guard's gun and shoot himself in the head.

As to what the unfortunate employee saw is only described in the scant scribbles he left in his note taking, a Russian phrase that roughly translates to "the sights of Hell bring its viewers back in." As to what he saw and as far as we know, no one else has ever seen it. Purportedly, further efforts by subsequent Disney employees to access the footage have been unsuccessful, the only result being their prompt termination. The footage has been allegedly deleted from that very computer, and the film safely ensconced back in the Disney vault for no one to ever see again.

Chapter 2: Strange & Curious Toys

# The Haunted Monkey

*"That monkey is haunted!"*

So declared Misty when she found the monkey once again on the mantle in the living room. Misty had secretly thrown the monkey away because it made her nervous. She suspected her brother had found the toy in the trash and taken it back out, placing it on the mantle to taunt her, but she wasn't sure. She decided to leave the monkey alone.

Misty and her family moved into the home in upstate New York in the summer of 1996. It was an older home that had sat empty for some time. Misty, along with her parents and younger brother had moved from the city and were all excited about being in a more rural area.

The house was dirty and in need of some repairs, but it was spacious, and both Misty and her brother would now have their own rooms. Misty's brother Robert was only ten at the time. On their first day in the new house, he set about exploring and found a toy monkey on a shelf in his closet. He loved the toy right away, even though it was aged and dirty. Robert was not a typical boy and had never taken to many toys, so when he showed the monkey to his mother with joy on his face, she told him he could keep it.

The monkey was an old wind-up toy with a pair of cymbals it would bang together. Misty's father tinkered with it to see if he could get it to operate, but he finally declared the mechanism to be too old and rusted to function anymore, so the monkey just sat with cymbals spread wide and a smile on its face.

Misty had read a scary story, or seen a movie or television show that had such a monkey in it, and because of this she found it unsettling. Robert was always leaving the monkey lying around the house. Misty would come in to watch television, and there was the monkey, sitting on the mantle staring at her.

Things took a creepy turn when she sat on the couch one Saturday reading a book. Everyone else was outside and the house was quiet. The silence was promptly broken by the sound of the monkey's crashing cymbals. Misty leapt off the sofa in fright and looked at the toy. The cymbals had stopped and the figure returned to its normal resting position. Misty felt a cold chill and immediately rushed outside. Her mother was sitting in a chair out front and she told her what had just happened.

*"Oh dear, it's probably just your imagination. Your father looked that toy over and said that it couldn't possibly work anymore."*

Her mother's words only agitated her, because she knew what she had heard. Before she could further argue the point, the phone started ringing and her mother got up to answer it. A few minutes later, Misty's mother came to the door and called everyone to come inside.

Something was clearly wrong. In tears, Misty's mother informed the family that her father had just passed away at his home in the Midwest. Misty rushed to her room and broke down in tears. She was even more disturbed by the passing because she just knew that the monkey's clanging cymbals had somehow announced the death.

The next night, Misty threw the monkey in the trash, angry and afraid that the toy had something to do with her grandfather's passing. But the next morning, there sat the grinning toy in its spot on the mantle. Misty declared the toy haunted but her parents simply thought she was distraught at the loss of her grandfather.

Six months later, the monkey's cymbals banged together again. Once again, Misty was the only one to hear them, and once again, a family death was announced immediately afterwards. While Robert still loved the monkey, to Misty the little toy was a harbinger of doom.

She forgot about the monkey when she moved away to go to college, but she faced it again when home visiting. The occasion was a somber one as her brother Robert had been killed in an accident. Sitting in the living room, she started at the monkey, wondering if it's cymbals had tapped together to signal Robert's death. To her the monkey didn't look as happy as it used to.

Misty's family eventually moved away from the home and retired out of state. When she helped her parents pack the house up, she couldn't bear to throw the monkey away, it had been too special to her brother. So Misty is now the reluctant owner of the toy. On occasion, she hears the voice of her brother. Perhaps it's her imagination, or perhaps his spirit is somehow attached to the little toy.

The monkey now sits quietly on a shelf in her home. Beside it is a picture of her brother, a painting of Jesus and an antique cross passed down from family members. Whenever she looks at the monkey, Misty thinks of Robert and prays she never hears those grim cymbals bang again.

Chapter 2: Strange & Curious Toys

# Her Baby Lamb

When it comes to haunted toys, it's not a surprise that they often seem to be tied to some tragic story of a child lost too soon. This story is no different.

There was a six-year-old girl named Cindy who never parted ways with her beloved baby lamb. Cindy loved her stuffed toy so much that the lamb displayed the wear and tear from the child's constant care and attention. Cindy's lamb was her most precious possession. Unfortunately, as one might guess, our story takes a turn for the worst. While young Cindy was crossing the street with her treasured lamb in her hands, a cab struck down the child. Thrown from her hands, the lamb was lost in the chaos as the medics tried diligently to save the child's life.

The next day the grieving parents returned to the spot where they lost their daughter in search of her baby lamb. Cindy's mother wanted her child to be buried with her favorite toy, but the search turned up nothing, and it seemed the toy was lost forever.

It was the day after Cindy's funeral when her parents discovered the baby lamb sitting on their front porch. Relieved the toy was found, they brought it into the house and placed it on their child's bed.

The next day Cindy's mother discovered the baby lamb sitting in front of the TV as if waiting for a favorite show to start, something Cindy had looked forward to every morning. Her mother picked up the lamb and took it back to Cindy's former room, only later to find the lamb sitting on a table in her playroom.

During the next few months Cindy's parents continuously found the lamb in various spots throughout the house, always in locations they knew they hadn't placed the toy. The family dog seemed to react to the toy as well. Excited barking would fill the rooms and the family would discover the lamb in a new place. The dog would run around the house as if chasing shadows that couldn't be seen - a familiar game played by the two when Cindy was alive. Right away, the mother knew it was her child returning home with her baby lamb.

Wanting to learn as much as she could, the mother's curiosity led her to seek help from the paranormal field. One investigator suggested trying audio recordings around the baby lamb to see if Cindy was trying to say something. It was while reviewing these recordings they obtained a child's distorted voice giggling, and what sounded like efforts of trying to talk to her mother.

During another of their recording sessions, the investigator captured the sound of Cindy crying. Immediately afterwards, the investigator picked up the lamb to move it and discovered the stuffed toy had a wet spot. The mother believes Cindy's tears caused the wet spot.

Late one evening, the mother awoke from her sleep. She felt a calling to her as she made her way to Cindy's bedroom where she found the baby lamb tucked under the covers of Cindy's bed. The mother reached down only to feel a chill run down her back. At that moment, the child's mother noticed a faint outline of her beloved Cindy standing in the room, holding her baby lamb. Before her mother could reach out to hug her one last time, the ghost of Cindy was gone.

Chapter 2: Strange & Curious Toys

# The Pokémon Panic of '97

December 16, 1997: 12,000 schoolchildren in Japan experienced physical problems ranging from nausea to seizures. The cause of the large-scale distress? An episode of the Pokémon cartoon.

Pokémon is a cultural phenomenon that has spread around the world, spawning countless cartoons, toys, comics, games, movies, trading cards and much, much more. In recent years the Pokémon Go app has given a whole new breath of life to the franchise, with frenzied crowds running around trying to "catch them all."

In 1997 the Pokémon fad had already taken firm hold in Japan and was just growing in popularity around the globe when the strange incident occurred.

The episode of Pokémon in question was number 38 (titled Dennou Senshi Porigon). Sometime during the episode, flashing lights filled the screen. Around thirty minutes later, worried parents began rushing their children to hospitals. Reports indicate around 600 to 700 kids in total were taken in for emergency care. Symptoms varied and ranged from nausea and vomiting to dizziness, trouble seeing and even seizures. The media picked up on the incidents and news stations quickly rushed to cover the story. In their excitement, some news programs replayed the clip of flashing lights from the cartoon, causing even more cases of children being taken in for medical care, and the Pokémon panic seemed to be spreading.

According to the newspaper "Yomiuri Shimbun":

*"Children went into a trance-like state, similar to hypnosis, complaining of shortness of breath, nausea, and bad vision...Victim's families reported that children passed out during the broadcast, went into convulsions, and vomited."*

The number of children reportedly affected shot up to 12,000 cases by the next day, with some news sources reporting an even higher number. Parents were frightened and outraged, calling on TV Tokyo to implement better controls over content and to place warnings on the cartoon. Some even wanted intense animations blocked completely. Even the Prime Minister of Japan spoke up about the incident in a public statement:

*"Rays and lasers have been considered for use as weapons. Their effects have not been fully determined."*

Nintendo, the giant behind the popular Pokémon video games was anxious to protect its big money-maker. They quickly sent a spokesman out to explain to the public that the only link between the cartoon and its games was the characters, so there was nothing to worry about in terms of the games. Despite the statements, company sales dropped about five percent on the Tokyo stock market. Shortly after the panic, TV Tokyo issued an apology and suspended the program stating it would investigate what may have induced the seizures and other ill effects.

Officers from the National Police Agency questioned the cartoon's producers, looking into the production process itself to determine what had occurred. Health and Welfare officials held an emergency meeting and discussed the case with various experts and doctors from local hospitals. Various testimonies from both children and their parents were taken into consideration. Many of the statements were very similar in description:

*"As I was watching blue and red lights flashing on the screen, I felt my body becoming tense. I do not remember what happened afterward."* Said a 15-year-old interviewed by Asahi Shimbun.

Ten-year-old Takuya Sato stated: *"Toward the end of the program, there was an explosion, and I had to close my eyes because of an enormous yellow light like a camera flash."*

Experts stepped in and attributed the incidents to photosensitive epilepsy, a case wherein bright, flashing lights trigger symptoms like those reported during the panic. Epilepsy experts were skeptical about the explanation, pointing out that photosensitivity is only estimated to be present in approximately 1 in 5,000 people. How then could 12,000 children suddenly have this condition?

Video outlets began pulling previous episodes of the show from their shelves. TV Tokyo issued a statement that it was placing a warning label on past Pokémon episodes as a precaution. But despite the mass scare, it wasn't long before both children and parents were calling for a return of the beloved cartoon. By April, Pokémon returned to the airwaves. The fear it seemed, had passed. Questions remained, however. While many people accepted the photosensitivity explanation, skeptics attributed the panic to mass hysteria.

Mass hysteria is usually triggered by extreme and sudden stress that is converted into physical illness. Friends and family who witness such incidents are often "infected" with the condition, resulting in a chain reaction and a larger number of people suffering a similar but unexplainable condition.

This has in fact become the accepted explanation for the Pokémon panic, but is it accurate? Mass hysteria is usually dependent on those affected being in close quarters and proximity, where they can witness each other developing the symptoms. This was far from the case in this incident, as the children were mostly in their homes and spread throughout the country. Additionally, adults were apparently not affected by the panic, other than demonstrating their concern for the children.

Amidst all the scramble to determine the cause of the panic, there were various other theories. One proposed that the cartoon itself was haunted. It was speculated that some malicious spirit, perhaps a vengeful ghost, had entered the airwaves and struck out at an opportune moment when thousands of children were glued to their televisions. This supernatural attack may have caused a spiritual sickness that affected a large portion of the kids immediately and simultaneously.

Another researcher believed the whole thing was a massive experiment in mind control, or, a visual/audible weapon meant to disorient people on a massive scale.

*"Millions of people sit and watch television for hours on end. It's not hard to imagine that somewhere along the way, some government group has looked at ways to use that against the population. If they weaponize something that can be sent over the airwaves, they could incapacitate a huge segment of the population without lifting a finger. It's a scary prospect, but I think it's a possibility."*

Curiously, the episode of Pokémon in question involved the characters entering a computer and encountering a fighter named Polygon. Once the battle ensues, Pikachu uses his electrical powers to stop a "virus bomb" which results in the series of bright, flashing lights.

Coincidence, conspiracy or ghost? You decide, but bear in mind, the next time you turn on a cartoon, there may be a ghost in the machine, or something even worse behind the signal.

Chapter 2: Strange & Curious Toys

# Chapter 3:
# It's Only A Game

## The Haunted NES

Since their introduction, video games have been on the Christmas list of children far and wide, and electronic games have become firmly rooted in the modern age. What started out as large, bulky consoles has now evolved into handheld gadgets and everyday items. It should come as no surprise that along the way video games and ghostly legends would cross paths.

In March, 2005 An eBay dealer out of New York by the name of Joe Cascron listed a Nintendo Entertainment System (NES) for sale on the popular auction site. It was considered a vintage game and there was certainly a market for such things, but this game system came with an additional caveat; supposedly it was haunted.

Per the original eBay listing by Cascron:

*"I've been an eBay seller in the field of vintage games for close to a year. I've exchanged hundreds of video game related items, new and used, and still do till this day, but I have never experienced anything like this or even remotely similar. I don't feel threatened by this, supernatural or whatever it may be, but I do not feel exactly comfortable with it either. Up for auction is what I would call a haunted, vintage, video game system, the Nintendo NES. I don't really like using the word 'haunted' when describing this, considering the first thing you would think about is something from a horror movie, but I really can't come up with another way to explain it."*

Naturally, the listing drew some interest, no doubt due to the classic nature of the game system — and the claims of the console being haunted. Cascron said he had little information about the origins of any possible haunting, other than the information he received from the thrift shop owner:

*"There is a local thrift store here in Brooklyn, NYC that I've been doing*

business with for some years now. About a month and a half ago, I made one of my visits to the shop and found this '80s Nintendo system. When I purchased this unit, I asked the owner of the shop about who brought the system in, and what he actually told me was that a gentleman had donated it that same morning and said 'It was just sitting in his attic,' and according to him, it supposedly belonged to his son who passed away years ago. At first I thought the guy was joking with me like he usually does, so I really didn't think much about it at the time."

Cascron further stated that he went back to the shop two weeks later to ask more questions about the Nintendo and the man who had brought it in. Unfortunately, the store owner had no other details he could add to the story. Technically the game system appeared to be in good working condition for a vintage item, with only an occasional "blinking" on the game screen. But something was not right:

"I brought this system home, and on the first night of playing, about ten minutes into the game, I began hearing sounds similar to human voices, mumbling to the background music of the television. Naturally I thought it may have been static or something to that effect, or maybe it somehow interfered with a truck driver's CB radio system, so I didn't pay much attention to it. But it continued throughout the entire time I was playing; stop for a minute or two, then start again. It got to the point where I went really close to the TV, I paused the game to try to hear it a little better, but then it would get silent. When I would un-pause it, there it would go again. I know it sounded like there was a conversation going on but I couldn't make out any of the words."

Cascron claimed he had no belief in ghosts or spirit communication. He writes that other odd glitches started to occur with the system as he played it. The game would sometimes pause at critical moments and the character on screen would not be under his control. He tried multiple controllers but experienced the same issues. He invited various friends and family members to try the system out and they too had odd experiences. His fiancé was so disturbed by the behavior of the system she stopped letting him turn it on when she was in the house. Cascron also stated his cat wouldn't go near the Nintendo, and the animal started running wildly around the house at night, something it had never done in the eight years he'd had her. Finally he was ready to be rid of the thing:

"I sincerely believe there may be some form of strong connection or attachment between this system and its previous owner. The reason I am listing this…to be honest, it's starting to freak me out, as well as the people *around me. I don't feel threatened; I just don't understand it and I'm not exactly comfortable with keeping this in my home. So, at the request of friends and loved ones, I'll be going my separate ways with this system, regardless if it's an actual supernatural presence or everyone is just being paranoid. I'll be putting this unit up for one penny without a reserve price; if you're the high bidder, the unit and everything with it will be yours."*

The Nintendo sold to a man named Jerry in Minnesota for $225.53. Jerry was a game designer with an interest in the paranormal so the combination of the two fascinated him at the time. He started a blog with the intent of studying the system and documenting any possible supernatural activity around it. However, the blog only amounted to a handful of posts. Along the way, Jerry sent the game to a writer for "Electronic Gaming Monthly" who promptly wrote a story making fun of the entire situation.

However, Jerry later confirmed he had not sent the real haunted Nintendo because he didn't want to risk it being damaged or lost. Instead he'd sent a duplicate, knowing full well the intent of the writer.

So what happened to the haunted system? In a 2015 interview Jerry confirmed he still had the item but he'd had little time to continue his experiments with it. He noted after his blog, he did experience some odd glitches in the game and its controllers, but nothing in terms of extreme paranormal evidence.

Jerry's research partner moved away and on a personal level, Jerry got very busy with day to day life, work and marriage. Today the haunted NES sits at Jerry's house gathering dust. Perhaps the spirit is quietly waiting for someone new to delve into its haunted, electronic world.

# The Midnight Man

Urban legends have to start somewhere, right? Many believe the origins of the so-called Midnight Man or Midnight Game is found in old pagan rituals. These events were employed to intimidate or punish those who dared to disobey the laws and traditions of the gods. Forget death, banishment, or, the messy work of purifying the "unclean" by pouring bull's urine over them, let's just scare them to death.

The questions and the roots of the Midnight Man have gone unanswered. The game has become a popular activity for many thrill-seeking participants; however, many have walked away with mental scars or physical injuries as they try to avoid encountering the Midnight Man.

If you choose to summon the Midnight Man, which you do at your own risk, please follow these instructions very carefully.

More than one player can partake in this game. However, all players must perform the summons individually. Once he has been beckoned, your only goal is to avoid running into him throughout the darkness that surrounds you.

Before beginning, each player will need the following supplies:

- 1 candle
- Book of matches or a lighter
- A piece of white paper
- A pen or pencil
- A sharp needle
- Sea Salt

Also, the location requires a wooden front or back door.

The Summoning Instructions:

1. Begin just before midnight.
2. Write your full name – first, middle, and last – on the white piece of paper.
3. Then prick your finger and squeeze a small drop of

blood onto the paper, allowing it to soak in.

4. Turn off all light sources in your home, leaving your environment completely and utterly dark.

5. While outside, in front of the wooden door, tape or tack the paper with your name and blood on the door. Each person then lights their individual candle and holds it in their hand.

6. Just seconds before midnight strikes, begin knocking on the door 22 times. By the time you finish, it should be right on the midnight hour. Open the door; step inside the house or building, then blow out the candle. Once all the candles are blown out then close the door behind you.

7. At this moment you need to immediately relight your candle.

8. Now, the game has begun as you have just invited the Midnight Man to come play. Some who have played this game claim they have heard the Midnight Man knock on the door waiting for an answer. However, don't answer — whatever you do. It's only a trick for him to catch you right away.

Throughout the night remember to:

1. Always keep your candle burning and in hand with your salt and matches or lighter in your pocket as you move about.

2. Always keep moving. If you should stop, the Midnight Man will be able to catch you.

3. If your candle happens to go out, you must relight it within ten seconds if you wish to continue moving about the rooms or to escape the Midnight Man himself. Otherwise, immediately surround yourself in a circle of sea salt and remain there until 3:33 am.

Ending the game:

At 3:33 am the Midnight Man is called back to his dwellings. It is now safe to stop moving or to step outside your circle of salt.

Signs the Midnight Man is near

- You will encounter sudden drops in temperature.
- You will hear low grumbling whispers with no noticeable source.
- You will see a human-like shadowy figure standing in the darkness.
- You will hear footsteps that follow you around.
- He will call out your name.
- Your candle will mysteriously go out.

If you experience any of these, it's suggested you leave the room immediately. Still, remember to relight your candle within the ten seconds or he will get you. Or quickly surround yourself in a circle of sea salt or again he will get you. There appears to be no other way to end the game but to survive until 3:33 am.

Whatever you do...

- DON'T leave the house or building
- DON'T turn on any lights
- DON'T use a lighter or a flashlight instead of a candle
- DON'T use someone else's blood
- DON'T go to sleep
- DON'T provoke the Midnight Man

As to what happens when the Midnight Man catches someone, several accounts differ. The popular belief is he will haunt with hallucinations of the person's deepest darkest fears. Some say he tortures by squeezing his preys' organs causing so much pain they can only wish death would come quickly. However, this only lasts until 3:33 am when his reign of terror ends.

So if you've lasted that long and the Midnight man hasn't found you, it seems you've won the game. Nonetheless, let's just hope he's really gone for good.

Knock, knock...

## Hide and Seek, Alone

We can all reminisce back to our childhood and remember the games we played. One game I recall was "Out to see the Ghost tonight." Very similar to the classic Hide and Seek, but only played at night or in the dark. Here, one person (the ghost) counts out loud the hours of the day until they've reached midnight. At the same time, the others would hide from the ghost. At the call of midnight the "ghost would wander around trying to find their victims one by one and when they were found, you yelled "YOU'RE DEAD!" until they were all found. A game any future ghost hunter would enjoy. However, there is one game of Hide and Seek most would be too frightened to play, especially ALONE.

The game is called Hitori Kakurendo, a dangerous Japanese hiding game that involves a possessed doll, a sharp knife and only yourself. I would never encourage anyone to tempt fate. But I feel a warning should be applied whenever taking matters into your own hands when dealing with unknown spirits.

Hitori Kakurendo is a form of a ritualistic game that calls upon spirits or what some believe are demons that will seek you out. The game truly pushes your senses to the limits, playing cat and mouse with the haunted doll while hiding in the darkness and waiting for some sort of sign of the doll drawing closer and closer.

To play the game you need a doll you can cut open and fill with uncooked rice, a needle and red thread, a cup of salt water, a knife, an AM/FM radio and a small-enclosed space where you can hide.

Follow these steps very closely:

1. Cut open the doll and remove any filling and replace it with the uncooked rice. Asian cultures believe rice will attract spirits.

2. A clipping of your hair or fingernails must be placed inside the doll as well. By doing this, you are now binding the doll to you and you alone.

3. Take the needle and red thread and sew the doll up. Also use any extra thread to wrap around the doll. This signifies blood and will bind the spirit to the doll.

4. Fill a sink or bathtub with water.

5. Find your hiding spot and place the cup of salt water there.

6. Now you must choose a name for the doll. It is believed that naming the spirit gives the entity more power.

7. The game begins at 3AM. At this time you stand next to the sink or bathtub holding the doll and say "your name is \_\_\_\_ " out loud. Then whisper into its ear three times "(YOUR NAME) is it!"

8. Submerge the doll in the sink or tub. Then turn the radio onto a static channel with the volume up loud enough that you can hear it in your hiding space. You will then grab the knife and start turning off all the lights in the house as you make your way to your hiding spot.

9. Once in your hiding location, close your eyes and start counting to 10.

10. After counting, return to the doll with the knife in hand.

11. Confront the doll and say " I found you, (Dolls Name)!" then stab the doll three times with the knife.

12. Now it's the dolls turn. Remove the doll from the water and whisper three times in its ear "Now (Dolls Name) is it!" place the doll back in the water with the knife by its side.

13. Now run quickly to your hiding spot and wait patiently.

If all that wasn't creepy enough, by this point those brave enough to have played the game reported hearing the sounds of tiny feet running around the house, the radio static sound changing or turning off, a child's laughter, and strange noises of knocking on walls. Others have even said they have experienced dramatic temperature changes, horrific smells, followed by the feeling of being touched or pulled.

Once you feel the presence of the doll approaching, you MUST end the game. You do this by quickly taking a mouth full of the saltwater, but DON'T swallow it. It must remain in your mouth until you find the doll. It is also important that you don't look behind you. Keep calm for you may be surprised to find the doll is not where you left it. And now you must find it before all the salt-water leaks from your mouth. Once the doll is found now spit the salt water onto the doll and say three times "I win!" after doing so, now remove the red thread. This will unbind and free the spirit bringing the ritual to an end.

But to be sure the game is completely done, dry the doll and discard it. Some have burned the doll, while others have buried it.

## The Berzerk Curse

The 80s launched big changes for children of the decade. Technology was finally in their reach as toys developed into computers and video games. Atari was making headway, debuting in just about every household as the digital age was born, and every kid wanted a piece of it.

It was in the 1980s that Stern Electronics developed the video game called Berzerk, a game that takes players through a maze, shooting at robots as they make their way to battle the arch-nemesis, Evil Otto.

At first it seems nothing out of the ordinary, very much like all the other video games being mass-produced at the time. However, one interesting fact behind the game was that it was inspired by an employee's dream. Alan McNeil dreamt about a detailed black-and-white video game in which he had to fight off robots.

Today, Berzerk lives on through history, not for being an award-winning game or leading the way for any new developments, but rather it's known for killing off the people who played the game. Legend has it if you were one of the players that reached one of the top ten scores, you might not live to brag about it. And there is some truth to be told when it comes to this story.

In Calumet City, Illinois, there was a place called Friar Tuck's Game Room. A huge round wooden door marked its entrance, as the place was themed as if you were stepping back in time to the days of Robin Hood and his Merry Men, complete with wrought iron lamps and stained glass windows. Here, on Saturday, April 3, 1982, 18-year old Peter Bukowski played his last game of Berzerk.

That day Peter arrived at the game room around 8 pm excited to get his hands on Berzerk, a game he was known to spend most of his time playing. That night he reached two high scores in less than 20 minutes. He put his initials on the screen and decided to go for one more game before calling it a night. Again he was among the top 10 high scores. He put in his initials and stepped away only to come crashing to the ground. Peter was unresponsive as the attendant began CPR while they waited on an ambulance. For some strange reason he couldn't be brought back to consciousness. Peter was rushed to a local hospital where he was pronounced dead on arrival.

His story gained popularity as rumors emerged on how a video game killed an innocent boy. Arcade owners were asked to remove the game immediately from their stores, and schools announced that children were advised to restrain themselves from playing the game.

Ever since video games came to be, parents and even scientists have questioned how video games impact people in the long term. I'm sure we can remember how older generations believed Rock and Roll was the work of the devil and influenced children to do bad things. Unfortunately, this became a similar situation. Do video games carry some supernatural power?

Technology was evolving at such a rapid rate it was hard to keep up with the side effects they may have had on unsuspecting players. Even in today's studies, it is still questioned if violent games help stimulate vicious urges or promote them.

Nevertheless, our story must go on. It wasn't too long after Peter's ill-fated encounter that rumors of other cases started popping up throughout the media, claiming others died playing the doomed Berzerk game. One widespread story involved a young man of 19 named Jeff Dailey, who died when he reached the high score of 16,660. However, his case was later proved false, and his story was removed from the Berzerk Curse.

Yet there is still a story to be told about that particular arcade game that never left the old Friar Tuck's Game Room. On March 20, 1988, an adolescent of 17 named Edward Clark Jr., played the same Berzerk game Peter played years before. It seems there was a bit of a confrontation with another young man, and 16-year-old Pedro Roberts claimed he had dibs on the game before Edward cut in. It seems the two were both equal in their stubbornness and refused to let the matter go. Within a short amount of time, a fight developed between the two and store clerks stepped in and made the young men leave. However, Pedro had a score to settle and waited in the alley just outside the shop. When Edward made his way outside, Pedro rushed Edward, stabbing him in the heart and killing him.

So yes, two young men did indeed die after playing the exact same arcade game in the exact same room in what was once Friar Tuck's Game Room. While the claims that a video game can kill remains up for debate, the published game might be safe to play. However, that specific arcade game seems to offer bad luck to the young men eager to play it.

Chapter 3: It's Only A Game

As to the fate of that model of the arcade game Berzerk, no one knows. Once Nintendo, Sega, PlayStation and Xbox hit the market with home systems, the arcade days faded into the darkness, taking along with them places like the old Friar Tuck's Game Room. For all we know the game could still be out there preying on young men, but their unfortunate stories have yet to be told.

# Bloody Mary

It's an age-old ritual that's become a creepy sleepover game especially appealing to young girls. It's called "Bloody Mary."

The "game" allows a questioner to summon the spirit of Mary Worth who may or may not provide a glimpse into the future. The modern version requires standing in front of a mirror while holding a lit candle. The person wishing to summon Mary spins around three times and then chants "Bloody Mary, Bloody Mary, Bloody Mary." Purportedly, the face of Mary will appear in the mirror. Her appearance may be the face of a young woman, or a hideous display rivaling the grim reaper itself. Part of the gamble of playing the game involves Mary's nature. She may be benign and give the seeker a glimpse of their future spouse, or she may be malevolent and give a glimpse of death. Dare you take the chance?

Susan did when she was fifteen years old.

She went to a sleepover along with three other girls at a friend's house. The normal antics ensued, talk of boys and music, and finally, a game of truth or dare. When it was her turn, Susan chose a dare. The other girls challenged her to play Bloody Mary. Thrusting a candle into her hand, they sent her to the bathroom to stand before the mirror and chant the dreaded name.

Susan performed the required ritual and waited. She felt as if she stood in front of the mirror for ages and decided nothing was going to happen. Just as she turned to leave the room, her candle started to flicker. She turned back to the mirror, only to behold a horrible face staring back at her. It was a disfigured woman with a frightening smile. Susan screamed, much to the delight of the other girls in the adjoining room, and dropped the candle. In a panic, she scrambled to the light switch and flipped it on.

The candle was on the floor, a splash of wax on the tile. Looking up slowly, Susan found that there was nothing unusual in the mirror, only her own face. But something wasn't quite right. Looking closely at her reflection, Susan saw a long scratch going down the left side of her face, as if a sharp fingernail had traced a line from the corner of her eye all the way down to her neck. Had some spirit come through the mirror and attacked Susan? Years later, she still remembers the incident and has no explanation for her experience.

Bloody Mary arose as a popular adolescent party game in the 1960s, but it wasn't until the 1970s that folklorists started recording examples and variations of the game. Other versions include "Mary Worth," Mary Wales," and "Hell Mary."

Somewhere along the way, a backstory became attached to the bloody apparition. Legend says Bloody Mary was a woman named Mary Worth. Mary was a beautiful young woman who spent too much time admiring herself in the mirror. One day she suffered a terrible accident that left her face permanently disfigured. Mary's parents removed many of the mirrors from the home and forbade their daughter from looking at her reflection. Curiosity eventually got the best of Mary and she snuck into a room with a mirror to get a look at herself. When she saw her reflection, Mary broke out into terrible screams and went mad. She walked into the mirror and never returned to the physical world.

There's a large body of folklore attached to the Bloody Mary legend and it has roots in ancient forms of mirror divination rituals. Older versions of the Bloody Mary game required a woman to walk up a flight of stairs backwards while holding a candle and a hand mirror in a darkened house.

With the rise of contemporary versions of Bloody Mary, the process has taken a darker turn. Sometimes Mary is said to appear covered in blood. She may scream at the seeker or even try to hurt them by scratching at their eyes or trying to strangle them. Some believe Mary even attempts to steal souls.

Is it imagination? The fantastic imaginings of young girls hyped up with excitement and expectation? Or is there something more to the legend? Has some dark spirit answered the call, taking the form of Bloody Mary, waiting quietly on the other side of a mirror's void for an opportunity to make contact with an innocent seeker?

Dare you take the risk to chant Bloody Mary?

Chapter 3: It's Only A Game

## The Hosting Game

There's nothing like hosting the perfect party, cranking up the music and having a good time with your friends. But what happens when your friends don't show up? Or the DJ's a miss as well? Don't worry, it seems there's a few guests that you can count on if you summon them to fill the void.

The Hosting game is undoubtedly a very different kind of party. In it, you call on three menacing ghosts to entertain you, or are you entraining them? Either way, it's a party where "uninvited" guests crash and you just might want to steer clear of them as they may seek to prey upon you.

To start off, it's recommended that you be alone in the house. Some spirits don't like to appear when there's a group of friends around. It is also recommended you play the game at night, in complete darkness and in a small confined space, preferably a closet, when hosting your ghostly party.

Anybody wanting to screw around with something that has even a slightest chance of filling their house with vengeful spirits, or even worse, is asking for trouble, and we'd recommend rethinking your actions if considering playing this game.

Here is what's required:

A hosting room - small, dark, empty room with no windows; this should be a closet space, pantry or maybe even a bathroom. The room should be big enough for a single person to turnaround without touching anything. No outside light should be visible from inside the room.

- A pen and paper.
- An analog clock or watch. It must be a timekeeping device that emits NO light whatsoever.
- 3 matches.
- A flashlight or candle.

How to play:

- Turn off all sources that produce any noise. This includes phones, computers, TVs, etc.
- Turn on a light source in the room you are using as your hosting room. If it's without a light, use a candle or a flashlight.
- Start at the furthest point in the house from the hosting room. Go room to room turning off all the lights and

calling out "I'll be ready soon!"

- Once all the lights in the house have been turned off and you've ended back at the hosting room, take out the paper and write, "You are invited! A party, hosted by (your name). Takes place from (time you start - an hour from start time). Bring friends!"

- Place it on the floor in the middle of the room, and shut yourself in the room, calling out "I'm ready! Come on in!"

- Turn off the light and turn around, so you are facing the darkened room. The door should be behind you.

- Take out the three matches and hold them in your hand.

- Wait and listen for a few moments in silence.

At this point, those who have played the game have heard a door open and close or the sounds of someone walking around. If you hear someone or something, begin counting out loud. When you get to ten, strike the first match.

If the match does not strike on the first try, immediately strike the second one. If the second does not light on the first attempt, try the third one. If this also does not ignite right away, it is a sign that your invisible guests have arrived, and are in the room with you. Whatever you do, do not turn around, or pause for too long. Reach for the nearest light source and turn it on. The party is now over.

If the first match lights on the first strike, hold it until it burns down as far as you can bear. Greet your guests out loud, "I'm so glad to see you! Thank you for coming! You may enter the room."

Repeat this process for the next two matches; however, if any of them does NOT ignite on the first strike, your guests have gotten too close. You must turn on a light to chase them away, but this action will end the spook fest.

Strike the third match. If it does light right away, call out into the air "Now everyone is here!" and then count to ten again. If everything was done correctly, you will hear whispering or rustling. Some folks have reported hearing a whispering voice say "Thank you" or "Thanks" from behind them. Others have reported feeling a pressure or coldness in the room, indicating a strange presence.

Once you've completed lighting all three matches successfully and made your spooky guests feel welcome, you can begin to have some sort of interaction with them. Here you might ask questions into the air and ask the spirits to knock on something to respond. Some have witnessed objects moving on their own or disappearing and showing up again where the object was left.

Strange things will happen as the party kicks off. Several witnesses claim to see the room get darker and the feeling of being overwhelmed as the party carries on. However, make sure you never turn around or look over your shoulder. Also make sure the ghosts never get too close or touch you. If this should happen, that spirit could become attached to you, and you might never get rid of it.

Now's the time to keep track of the time. Once it becomes the time you indicated on your invitation for the party to end, say out loud, "Thank you for coming. Goodbye." The party has come to a close, and the game has ended. Afterward, it is now safe to walk about and turn on the lights.

It's recommended that you don't assume your guests have left the building. Once they've been invited in, it's really hard to get them to leave, even if you complete or abort the game. It is further recommended that you avoid any dark rooms in your home for the next few days as things start to settle down. But let's hope everything went well, and on your next invite, you might suggest to your unseen guests that they BYOB, or rather "bring your own boos."

Chapter 3: It's Only A Game

## Charlie Charlie

Imagine, if you can, the following conversation:

*"Hey! Let's summon a Mexican demon"*

*"Uh, what for?"*

*"Because it will answer all of our questions."*

*"Really? What's the demon called?"*

*"Charlie Charlie."*

*"There's a Mexican demon called Charlie Charlie and we can ask it any question we want?"*

*"Yeah, and it'll answer. Oh, one thing, we have to ask permission to stop asking questions and we're only allowed to stop if Charlie Charlie says we can stop."*

*"Wow, sounds fun, let's try it!"*

This may sound like something out of a B horror movie, or even a comedy routine, but it's actually a fad that went viral on the Internet in the spring of 2015. The game is called the "Charlie Charlie Challenge."

Full instructions, along with photos and videos to demonstrate flew around the Internet, posted to various sites to encourage people, especially children, to participate. Individuals uploaded videos of their success in summoning the demon along with commentary on the accuracy of Charlie Charlie's answers.

The "game" is fairly simple and involves drawing an equally armed cross on a piece of paper. By default, this creates four squares. In two of the squares, the word no is written, and in the other two, yes. Next, two pencils are placed over the drawn cross, one on top of the other.

A chant is used to bring forth the demon. Participants must ask Charlie Charlie if he is present. Purportedly, he announces his presence by causing the pencils to move. Once it has been ensured that he has been properly summoned, the participants can proceed to ask questions.

Answers are conveyed by the movement of the pencils that will indicate either a yes or no answer. According to the rules of the challenge, the demon has to give his permission before the session can be ended. It is claimed that not receiving Charlie Charlie's permission to stop can lead to a plague of paranormal activity and ill fortune.

The game spread at an amazing rate, going "mega-viral," topping Internet trends lists and becoming the most searched item in numerous countries around the world.

The main audience for the game was teenagers and pre-teen children. It was played at schools, playgrounds, and of course at late night sleepovers.

Strange reports started to roll in connected to the Charlie Charlie game. One site reported numerous deaths were caused by attempts to interact with the demon.

People posted photos of scratches and claw marks they claimed they had received from angering Charlie Charlie.

Priests and ministers began to issue warnings about the dangers of the game and the pitfalls of dabbling with demons, even in what appeared to be childish formats. As is often the case, this merely drew more attention to the whole Charlie Charlie challenge. More stories, more publicity, more people attempting to contact the demon.

Obviously, Charlie isn't a Spanish name and there's certainly not a Mexican demon bearing the moniker. As Maria Elena Navez of BBC Mundo so accurately stated:

*"Mexican legends often come from ancient Aztec and Mayan history, or from the many beliefs that began circulating during the Spanish conquest. In Mexican mythology you can find gods with names like 'Tlaltecuhtli' or 'Tezcatllipoca' in the Nahuatl language. But if this legend came after the Spanish conquest, I'm sure it would have been called 'Carlitos' (Charlie in Spanish). There's no demon called 'Charlie' in Mexico. Mexican demons are usually American inventions."*

As for the game itself, it seems to be a modern incarnation of an old Spanish paper and pencil game called "Juego de la Lapicera" (game of the pens). It's a simple game often played by Spanish schoolgirls to answers common questions of teenage angst such as "does he like me" and "who will I marry."

While this version of the game has been played for generations in Spain and parts of Hispanic America, it seems to have really started having an internet presence only in 2008, at which point the hashtag #CharlieCharlieChallenge was attached to it. It was relatively unnoticed until the spring of 2015 when an online tabloid published a fearful story about the dangers of the Mexican demon "Charlie Charlie." A couple of follow up reports, some online videos, and suddenly Charlie Charlie was "trending," zipping to the far corners of the web in rapid order.

Soon after the meme went viral on the World Wide Web, the muddy waters of the challenge became even more fogged when a movie studio jumped on the bandwagon and claimed credit for the sudden popularity of the game.

A viral marketing team for a film titled "The Gallows," claimed they were behind the online popularity of the Charlie Charlie stories. They released a clip from the film that featured one of the movie's characters taking part in the Charlie Charlie challenge. They even went so far as to claim they had created the idea of the game themselves as part of their marketing strategy. Deeper research quickly reveals this is not the case, since the game predates the film. Of note, there's no demon called Charlie in the film. Clearly, another case of the entertainment industry attempting to jump into a popular craze to increase profits.

The game caught the attention of many religious leaders concerned about the potential of dark forces and many of them made public statements. In a report from the Catholic News Agency, Vatican approved exorcist, Father Jose Antonio Fortea weighed in on the demonic game and issued a stern warning saying:

*"...the so called Charlie Charlie challenge, a game played on a simplified version of the Ouija board, poses a real danger as it involves the summoning of spirits. Players won't be possessed, but the spirit that has been summoned will stay around for awhile, and the game will result in other spirits beginning to enter into even more frequent communication."*

While the Internet fad has long passed, people continue to play Charlie Charlie. Can a simple pair of pencils balanced on each other really summon a demon? Many people continue to believe they can, and for those who are open enough to attempt contact with sinister, underworld forces, perhaps — just perhaps, this is the case.

Chapter 3: It's Only A Game

# The Possessed Doll Game

In many cultures, there is a drive to make contact with the afterlife. This can be for religious enrichment, spiritual guidance or just for entertainment purposes.

There's a game from Indonesia called Jelangkung that uses a form of channeling, séance, and a Ouija board, and dates back to an ancient manuscript from the 5th century. It originates from a Chinese game called Cai Lan Gong, which roughly translates to "Vegetable Basket Spirit" - a basket used to carry dolls. Followers believed the gods Poyang and Moyang were called upon by children and placed into dolls to act as a sort of prophecy device. This was done during the Moon or Mid-Autumn festivals.

The Indonesian culture created an adult version, removing the innocent approach and becoming a more disturbing way of channeling all manner of spirits into our world.

The idea is to summon a spirit into an effigy form of some sort, such as coconut dolls or a wooden puppet dressed in doll clothes. These possessed dolls were asked questions or to predict the future. Groups of people would hold the doll up to a blank piece of paper and guide the doll as it wrote down the answers.

Requirements:

- A doll of any sort
- Clay or dirt from a graveyard or cemetery
- Blank paper
- A pen, marker or crayon
- Tape
- Various types of flowers (rose, magnolia, jasmine, tuberose, Carnation, Dahlia, Daisy, lily, marigold)
- Fruit or snacks for an offering
- 1 drop of musk oil to be rubbed on the doll
- 1 drop of jafaron oil to be rubbed on the doll
- Myrrh, buhur maghribi and frankincense (to be burned while calling spirits)

The Chant:

Words must be spoken with the correct pronunciation. Below is the chant as it appears in Indonesian and English:

- In Indonesian: "Jelangkung, Jelangsat, di sini ada pesta,

pesta kecil-kecilan. Jelangkung, Jelangsat, datang tak diundang, pulang tak diantar."

- In English: "Jelangkung jelangsat, we have a party here, a small party. Jelangkung jelangsat, come uninvited, go undelivered."

Other Considerations:

- Play anytime between 10pm and midnight
- The group playing must be an odd number, at least 5 people (1 person chanting the spell, the others holding the doll by its feet)
- Play the game in an uninhabited room, preferably a haunted one.
- Better if played on nights with a full moon
- When the spirit arrives, the doll is known to move (such as wiggling or jerking around) or to become heavy.
- The Spirit is known to ask for something in return, usually they want blood from a chicken.
- Whatever you do, do not run away, pass out or scream when the spirit has made itself known.
- If you disrespect the spirit, they are known to possess you.

It seems there are a few different ways to play the game jelangkung. Some still use traditional ways, as others have adapted to newer practices. Either way, it's still played today but with strict warnings: Don't play this game if you don't have a strong faith or without being mentally prepared, because this game can cause emotional stress, mental break down, and some have even claimed death.

Here's how a more modern version is played. Take the writing utensil and tape it to one of the doll's hands. Then place the doll on a bed of cemetery dirt, with the offerings of food and flowers positioned all around the doll. Next, light the incense and begin rubbing the oils on the doll. Take two small pieces of paper and write, "yes" on one and "no" on the other, then place them on either side of the black pieces of paper.

Now, one person will do the chanting as the others hold the doll one inch off the dirt bed. As the chanting continues, those holding the doll wait until the doll moves or begins to feel heavy. Once this happens, the group will hold the doll by its feet and carry it over to the paper with the writing utensil touching the paper. Similar to using a planchette on a Ouija board, the doll will start to guide those holding it as it begins to write.

It is customary to ask the doll to introduce itself, after which it will allegedly write its name down. Some may ask how it died. After this, the players may ask whatever they want of the spirit, the answers to which it will either write on the paper or point to the "Yes" or "No" provided.

Some have asked for winning lottery numbers, what the future might bring or even about diagnosing illness. It seems you can pretty much ask anything you desire. The game is pretty simple and at this point, no different than using a Ouija board. But just like any other warning when tampering with spirit summoning, this can become extremely dangerous, especially when the spirit becomes angry and creates problems for those playing.

In September of 2014, 25 sixth grade male students of State Elementary School in Ciracas, East Jakarta were possessed when they played Jelangkung one evening. For forty minutes, they were running around crying and shouting hysterically. It was so out of hand they called on local religious leaders to offer up prayers to help calm down the troubled children.

Situations like this are not uncommon in Indonesian culture. There have been many cases in recent years where the spirits allegedly possessed players. Some of these spirits can be demanding, and if you can't or won't give them what they seek, they wouldn't go and all of those playing the game will never be the same.

So remember, when ending the game, you should always dismiss the spirit from the doll. If you forget and it is left trapped inside, trouble is in store for those who called upon it!

Chapter 3: It's Only A Game

# The Bath Game

Have you ever played Red Light, Green Light with a ghost?

Considered one of the most dangerous games ever played by children, the origin of the Bath Game comes from Japan and is called "Daruma-san."

The game involves summoning a ghost who follows you around throughout the day. This game presents supernatural threats, but also many dangers in the physical world. Common sense is required. To win, or simply to maintain your sanity, you must prevent the ghost from catching you.

Here are the rules of the game:

Before you go to bed for the night, get yourself ready for a bath.

Fill the tub with warm water, and turn off the lights so that it's completely dark.

Strip entirely naked, and sit in the middle of the tub facing the faucet or taps.

Close your eyes and wash your hair while repeating the words "Daruma-san fell down. Daruma-san fell down." over and over. If you are not sure, this is how it's pronounced "dah-roo-mah – san."

As you wash your hair, you should see the following in your mind's eye – the image of a Japanese woman standing in a bathtub. She slips and falls on a rusty tap, which impales her through the right eye and kills her.

Continue repeating, "Daruma-san fell down, Daruma-san fell down" until you finish washing your hair. Remember to keep your eyes closed the entire time.

At this point, some people claim to hear or feel the movement of the water behind them. Others have even sensed the water turn icy cold. But remember, it's very important you keep your eyes closed. Don't peek! You've just summoned her ghost. It's said the ghostly figure of a woman will rise out of the water behind you. You will feel her staring you down with her left eye as the right one bleeds from the damaged socket. Her head will be twisting just behind your right shoulder. Some claim to feel a burning sensation on their backs as they feel her long, black, tangled hair draping upon them, as her tattered and rotting clothes press up against their burning backs.

When you feel the presence of the ghost, ask aloud "Why did you fall in the bath?" Wait a few moments for her to reply. Some have heard her mutter something, but they can't understand her words.

Be careful with this next part. Stand up and get out of the bath as quick as you can without draining the tub, but your eyes must remain

Chapter 3: It's Only A Game

tightly shut. Move slowly and do not slip or trip. Be careful while doing this with a wet body, in a slippery room with your eyes closed! As you feel your way around, the ghost may try to trip you and bring about your death in a similar way to how she died. Once grounded, immediately leave the bathroom and shut the door behind you.

Once you are safely out of the bathroom, you may now open your eyes. However, don't return or let anyone else into the bathroom. This is her time to gather her strength and your time to try and enjoy a night's sleep – because as soon as you wake up tomorrow, the game commences.

The ghost is now going to follow you around, however, trying to look at her directly doesn't seem to work. Instead, glance over your right shoulder and to try to focus on her image. She's known to hide behind things. It's here you may see her shadow, or her hand gripping the corner of the wall. She'll try everything she can to get closer and closer as the day goes on. Don't let her catch you! If she's getting too close, shout "Tomare!" which means "Stop!" Then run away as quickly as possible, placing some distance between you and the ghost. All this is repeated throughout the day.

After you feel you've had enough and want to end the game, you must find her stalking shadow and shout "Kitta!" meaning "I cut you loose!" Then hold your hand out in front of you and swing it downward in a cutting or chopping motion. If done correctly, you will feel a heavy pressure fall off your back.

Nonetheless, you must end the game before midnight or the ghost will creep into your dreams to follow you, making it much easier for her to catch you.

Rules you must LIVE by:

- Do NOT open your eyes when the ghost first appears.

- Don't let her trip you while you get out of the bath.

- Don't re-enter the bathroom until morning.

- Do not drain the bathtub until morning.

- And whatever you do, DO NOT let her catch up to you!

Regardless of how intriguing this "game" might sound. There are some steps that are simply too dangerous. Just stepping out of a bathtub onto a wet floor can cause some serious injury or even possibly death. Please don't tempt fate by trying to summon this ghost. Dabbling into the unknown often results in unknown consequences.

Chapter 3: It's Only A Game

# The Ouija Board

It's considered by many to be the most evil "game" ever created. A tool for opening portals to hell and unleashing demons, an instrument of the devil himself!

It's called the Ouija board. Pronounced "wee-jee," the board's moniker is derived from the French and German words for yes. The board is a flat piece of wood painted with the letters of the alphabet, the numbers 0-9 and the words yes, no, hello and goodbye. There are also various graphics on the board such as a moon and sun. Also called a "talking board" or "spirit board," the instrument is used to communicate with the deceased, or, according to many researchers, whatever else may decide to come through.

The game is played utilizing a "planchette," a small, heart shaped piece of wood or plastic that is placed on the board. Participants place their fingers lightly on the planchette and call out to the spirits. According to the directions of the game, spirits will move the planchette around the board and spell out answers to any questions posed by the players.

Early marketing for the board often targeted couples as seen in this statement from the man who popularized the Ouija, William Fuld:

*"Ouija knows all the answers. Weird and mysterious. Surpasses, in its unique results, mind reading, clairvoyance and second sight. It furnishes never failing amusement and recreation for the entire family. As unexplainable as Hindu magic—more intense and absorbingly interesting than a mystery story. Ouija gives you entertainment you have never experienced. It draws the two people using it into close companionship and weaves about them a feeling of mysterious isolation. Unquestionably the most fascinating entertainment for modern people and modern life."*

Talking boards became extremely popular starting with the spiritualist movement. From the late 1800s into the 1950s, dozens of companies produced their own versions. The boards depicted mystical images such as pyramids and swamis, or graphics with darker tones, such as witches and devils.

In 1890, businessman Elijah Bond introduced the board commercially. They were regarded as a parlor game and with the ties to spiritualism, they were sure to be a money maker. Bond received a patent on the board/planchette combination the following year. Bond's employee William Fuld took over production of the boards and by 1901, Fuld was producing boards himself under the name "Ouija."

Using and marketing the name Ouija, Fuld reinvented the very history of the game claiming he had invented the talking board himself. His name has become synonymous with the Ouija. After his passing, Fuld's estate sold the business to Parker Brothers which was later acquired by Hasbro. The company continues to market the popular Ouija despite the controversies that surround the board.

Christian groups frequently speak out against any use of the Ouija, proclaiming the boards are clearly tools of the devil, and are dangerous in the hands of the young and unsuspecting, as doorways to demons can be opened by the instrument's use. The board, they say, can lead to demonic infestation and even worse, possession.

Horror films have made wide use of the Ouija, playing on its reputation as a method for summoning demonic entities as a plot device.

Paranormal investigators frequently state that Ouija boards are often a factor in negative hauntings.

Consider this case from an investigator in New York:

*"We were investigating a home in upstate New York where the family reported a lot of poltergeist type of activity. The incidents had been going on for about six months by the time we came in to check it out. We spent two nights in the house and very little happened so we were forced to say that we could find nothing was there. But the family called us back about three months later. They were desperate and said that things had gotten worse. This time they had some audio of weird voices so we went back for another investigation.*

*And this time, their teenage daughter was at home. She had been away on a school trip the first time we went in. And this time, when we interviewed her, after a lot of questions, we found out that she and her friends had been using a Ouija board. She claimed they were in contact with a spirt that was "helping" them with boys and things in school, giving them advice and psychic information. The spirit claimed it was one that had lived on the spot before the house was built.*

*It was a dark, dark situation and the teenager was having health issues as this whole thing had been developing. We felt it was a negative attachment coming through the Ouija board and that a religious authority needed to be called in before things became really, really bad."*

In this case, a priest was called in to cleanse the home, and the board was disposed of in a bonfire. No further disturbances were reported in the home after the cleansing and elimination of the Ouija board.

The story is similar to many accounts collected by investigators in recent years. Numerous paranormal experts advise strongly against any use of the Ouija, citing comments made by religious groups and noting that the boards open doorways to the demonic, or at the least, some kind of influence from unknown entities.

Some psychics and mediums advise strongly against use of the boards, and claim that use of the Ouija frequently leads to negative attachments and dark entities that plague people's lives, feeding on their energy and gaining more and more of a foothold in the physical world.

Others feel the board is simply an innocent tool for divination, and with proper precautions can be used to access psychic information.

Over the years, the Ouija board has gained a reputation of almost mythical power, with many reports of people attempting to destroy the boards after negative experiences. Purportedly, such evil-infused boards cannot simply be burned or broken and always manage to return if thrown in the trash.

Love it or hate it, the Ouija board is clearly here for the long run. Is it an innocent parlor game, or something much more sinister? Perhaps only those who place their hands on the planchette can truly answer.

#  Chapter 3: It's Only A Game

# GhostsЯuS

# Chapter 4:
# Where Children & Spirits Play

## Ghosts "R" Us

Sunnyvale, California, located in Santa Clara County, is one of the major cities that make up Silicon Valley. It's a town with a rich history, upbeat attitude, and a haunted toy store.

The haunted Toys "R" Us sits on property that once belonged to a man named Martin Murphy. Murphy owned a plantation on the site in the 1880s, and it was there he employed a preacher named Johnny Johnson. Johnny suffered from encephalitis and became known as "Crazy Johnny." Johnny fell in love with Murphy's daughter, Elizabeth, but the feelings were not mutual. Soon, he learned Elizabeth was planning to marry a lawyer and move away. Johnny was beside himself. After hearing the news, he went out to chop wood, swinging the axe wildly in his anger and missed his mark, cutting himself badly. The wound was fatal and Crazy Johnny bled to death. Ever since that day, Johnny's spirit has stayed on the land, searching in vain for Elizabeth, longing to tell her about his feelings and perhaps convince her to stay.

Even though the old farmland is now home to a Toys "R" Us, Johnny still roams about looking for his lost love. Store employees complain about unexplained noises, hearing their names called out by disembodied voices and feeling the touch of an invisible hand. Toys and other items have been known to launch themselves off shelves, and phantom footsteps have been heard echoing through the aisles of the store. Crazy Johnny even makes his way into the store's bathroom, opening and closing doors and turning on the water faucets.

The story of the haunted toy store was featured on an episode of "That's Incredible" in the early 1980s, and again in the 90's on a program called "Real Ghosts." However, the stories of ghostly activity date back to the 1970s when the store first opened.

Some employees at the store say they've seen the spirit of Johnny as a spectral figure wandering around the store. Sometimes he appears only as a shadow figure darting around the aisles, other times he's seen as the phantom of a man in his early 20's dressed in old-fashioned clothing.

There were so many tales of Crazy Johnny the staff decided to hold a séance and attempt to contact the spirit. During the session, a photographer named Bill Tidwell snapped photographs, hoping to catch evidence of the specter on film. One of his infrared shots did indeed capture what appears to be the silhouette of a man leaning against one of the store's shelves. The man is bathed in an intense, bright light. Some thought this was a sign Johnny was being called home, but his spirit still lingers among the toys.

One of the many accounts of Johnny's presence, recreated on the episode of Real Ghosts, involved a mysterious voice whispering out over the store's PA system:

"The Lord giveth, the Lord taketh away."

A sad statement from Crazy Johnny, still unable to deal with the loss of Elizabeth.

## More Toys, More Spirits

The Sunnyvale location of the Toys "R" Us isn't the only one reputed to be haunted. The chain's store in McAllen, Texas is also said to be the home of at least one ghostly presence.

One man worked at the store and spent most of his time in an office behind the children's clothing section. The room above his office was used for storage and filled with extra display shelves. The man would often hear footsteps coming from the room and the sound of things shuffling around. He would go upstairs to investigate and find no one in the room, yet he would have the sense that things had been moved around in the room.

When the gentleman asked other staff members about the odd occurrences, he found that other people had reported what sounded like a child running on the steps. The store's employees also told him there was a story that some time in the past, a little boy was playing on the stairs and fell. Since the stairs were metal, the boy was seriously injured. He passed out and was rushed to the hospital where he later died. It's believed the boy's spirit returned to the store, the last place he played in life and the site of his fatal accident.

Another story connected to the store involved the baby aisle on the girl's side. The aisle is filled with dolls, many of which are motion activated and either laugh or cry when someone passes in front of the doll's sensors. Employees report many nights when the dolls all suddenly start to laugh and cry at the same time, yet there would be no one— at least no living person— in the aisle.

Other staff members reported the same types of dolls suddenly going off in the rear stock room, again when no one was present. Perhaps the resident ghost had a good sense of humor.

It seems spirits, at least some of them, have a real affinity for toy stores because there are yet other reports of haunted Toys "R" Us locations around the country. The store in Eugene, Oregon is reported to be haunted by a spirit that likes to flip magazines off the shelves and make banging noises in the electronics section.

The location in San Jose, California is reportedly the site of a playful spirit known to make strange noises and play with various toys in the shop, especially at night after closing hours. The staff would come in to work and find toys randomly scattered on the floors after everything was cleaned and in order the night before.

Perhaps many of these ghosts are simply the spirits of lost, lonely children who have found a place that brings them a bit of joy in the afterlife. One thing's for sure, they'll have no shortage of things to play with!

Chapter 4: Where Children & Spirits Play

## The Tallmann Bunk Beds

In the spring of 1986 Allen and Debbie Tallmann found a small, three-bedroom ranch house, just over four years old on Larabee Street, the perfect home for their family. With two children and one on the way, they never imagined they would be responsible for disrupting a sleepy neighborhood in Horicon, Wisconsin.

The Tallmann's found themselves to be the root of a haunting hysteria that brought hordes of media, curious thrill seekers and raucous drunks determined to witness for themselves some of the bizarre rumors circling around their home. The incredulous accounts included stories of blood dripped from the walls of the house, dishes flying across the room, and even a snow blower operating on its own in front of a number of witnesses.

This exodus of curiosity seekers left the local police with their hands full, as hundreds flocked to Larabe St.; trespassing through neighbors' yards, climbing fences and peeking through their windows. Numerous arrests were made and street barricades set up by the police, but this still didn't stop them from coming.

Police Chief Douglas Glamann grew weary of the man-hours his officers put in to keep the spectators away. He met with the family determined to put an end to the foolishness disturbing the otherwise placid community. Surprisingly, upon hearing about the terrorizing and sleepless nights Allen and Debbie suffered over the previous nine months, he instead became convinced of their sincerity.

It was *Milwaukee Sentinel* reporter James B. Nelson that approached the police chief with an idea that might put an end to the rumors, by having the Tallmann's come forward with their tales of their paranormal frustrations. If the truth was out there, maybe it might nip the curious onlookers in the bud. It was agreed, as long as their identities were kept confidential, that the Tallmann's would share their story, and they provided an account most wouldn't believe.

It all started in May of 1987 when the Tallmann family purchased a second-hand bunk bed for $100 to accommodate their growing family. Moving the furniture upstairs marked the beginning of their nine months of horror. That first night their son experienced the clock radio taking on a life of its own, the knob on the radio turning randomly, arbitrarily switching the channels. The children that slept in the bunk beds became sick, and nightmares began to plague Debbie and her children's dreams nightly.

Debbie Tallman said *"I'd wake up in the night crying, and I'd ask Allen if I was going to have nightmares like this all my life. I would dream that my kids were dying, that Allen was dying, that my father was dying."*

For the next few months the couple heard inexplicable strange noises; a suitcase kept under the bunk bed kept sliding out by itself. The babysitter reported seeing a kitchen chair rock back and forth on its own. Doors would bang open and shut; strange voices would call out their names from nowhere creating more and more sleepless nights.

One day Alan was painting the walls in the basement when he was called up for lunch. He placed the brush on the table, only to find when he returned that the brush was now in the bucket standing straight up.

Their son who slept in the bunk bed claimed he saw a little old lady, really ugly, with long black hair and a glow about her resembling fire. Their daughter claimed to see this witch-like woman as well, saying that the figure hid 'behind her door.'

Frustrated, Allen couldn't stand watching his family suffer. One evening he walked throughout the house shouting at the top of his voice, *"Whatever is in our house, would you please leave my children alone? If you want to fight, fight me!"*

He later stated, *"I was like a wild man."*

A few weeks later on January 7, 1988, Alan returned home from his late shift at around 2 a.m. and heard an eerie, howling wind coming from the side of the house. As he investigated, a voice came out of the wind saying *"come here"* over and over again. Frightened, Allen turned back only to discover the garage on fire. *"Then it was glowing inside the garage, an orange red. There were flames coming out of the overhead door. There were two eyes in the windows."*

Rushing to the front door, Allen's lunch box was suddenly ripped from his hands and thrown across the living room as soon as he stepped inside the house. Ignoring the incident, Allen returned with a fire extinguisher, only to find the fire was gone, along with any visible signs of it ever happening.

By this time, Allen was sleeping in his daughter's room to provide some semblance of protection from the strange events. One night, as he slept at her bedside, he awoke to find a fog-like substance creep up from the floor, and a voice came emerged from the fog saying *"You're Dead."* Green eyes with blazing red pupils appeared from the mist, with flames emerging and just as quickly vanishing from sight.

Fearful of the strange things going on, the family invited Pastor Wayne Dobratz to bless the house. The pastor went on record stating he thought the spirits were not only evil, but down right demonic, saying that he felt the very presence of the devil.

On January 11, Alan had to work late and asked a relative to watch over the kids. The relative was a complete skeptic, and it was a rather bittersweet but exonerating surprise when Allen and Debbie discovered him screaming at a horrible female figure standing in the girl's bedroom.

Enough was finally enough, and Debbie loaded what she could into the family car, grabbing the kids and leaving the house, never to return.

On February 19, 1988, Nelson wrote an article updating those following the gruesome case. The Tallmann's, feeling the bunk beds may have been the root cause of all the insanity, destroyed the beds by burning them in a private landfill somewhere in the Horicon area, where they felt no one was likely to build a house. The exact location remains a secret to this day.

The Tallmann's kept their promise and never returned to the house. They continuously moved from motel to motel, afraid the media would track them down. The family went into hiding because skeptics claimed it was all simply a radical publicity stunt geared at garnering them money and fame. Farmers Home Administration, which held the mortgage, agreed to assume the title which cost the family about $3,000. They turned down a $5000 deal to tell their story to the *National Enquirer* and refused an opportunity to appear on the Oprah Winfrey Show. These are hardly the actions of someone trying to make a profit or seeking attention.

Just as in the famed Amityville Horror case, a family moved into their dream house, experienced horrific encounters, and eventually left everything they had behind in a desperate flight from the bizarre and terrifying. After leaving the house, they no longer had to endure any brushes with the darker aspects of the paranormal.

*Chapter 4: Where Children & Spirits Play*

# Toys in the Graveyard

Savannah, Georgia is renown as one of the most haunted cities in the United States. Nestled in the deep south, Savannah is rich in a haunted legacy that's endured since its early establishment as a British colonial bastion in 1733, throughout the horrors of the Civil War, with spooky tales continuing to color it's idyllic coastal charms through the modern era.

About ten minutes from the town's historic district lies Bonaventure Cemetery. The historic cemetery covers 160 acres and has become a famous spot for tourists, historians and those with an interest in the paranormal. The cemetery has always been a notable part of Savannah's history, but it really hit the map with the 1994 release of John Berendt's bestselling book, "Midnight in the Garden of Good and Evil." Featured on the cover was a stunning image by Savannah photographer Jack Leigh, depicting one of the cemetery's many statues, a sculpture known as the "Bird Girl." Between the book and the subsequent popularity of a movie adaptation, people began to flock to Bonaventure to see the infamous Bird Girl for themselves. Traffic at the site became so heavy the city had to eventually relocate the statue to prevent its destruction.

But the Bird Girl isn't the only famous grave site in the historic cemetery. Equally as popular is the final resting spot of a young girl who died in 1889, known as "Little Gracie." Little Gracie was Gracie Watson, born in 1883, the only child of W.J. and Frances Watson. The family was originally from Boston and moved to Savannah after Mr. Watson was hired as manager of the Pulaski Hotel. The Pulaski was a luxury destination for the wealthy, and considered one of the best in the south. Young Gracie became a popular figure at the hotel, capturing guest's attention with her bright eyes and warm nature. Visitors would frequently see her in the lobby singing and dancing happily.

Two days before Easter in 1889, little Gracie passed away. She had been suffering from pneumonia and couldn't hold on any longer. Many people in the city mourned the loss of the happy little girl and Gracie's father fell into a deep and profound depression. Gracie was laid to rest in a family plot in the Bonaventure Cemetery, and Mr. Watson had sculptor John Walz carve a monument for his beloved daughter. Walz used a photograph of Gracie to create the picture perfect image of her. This monument has caught the attention of visitors to the graveyard for over a hundred years, and has become one of the most visited grave sites in Savannah. But as you may have guessed, Little Gracie's story didn't end with her passing.

Gracie's mother Margaret claimed she could still hear Gracie laughing and playing under the back staircase of the hotel. Staff members reported hearing the girl's voice near the stairs, along with a low moaning and clanking coming from the basement. Some staff even refused to go down the steps after hearing the sounds. While alive, Gracie, if bored, would often go play beneath the back stairwell of the hotel. Apparently this behavior endured even after Gracie's unfortunate demise. The Pulaski Hotel was eventually demolished in 1957, but the site still boasts many ghostly sightings, Gracie among them. She has been frequently spotted in Johnson Square, a public space near the grand hotel's former location.

One curious incident occurred in the spring of 2002 when a Savannah tour guide was leading a group past the former hotel's site. She began to recount the story of Gracie to the group when she noticed an unfamiliar, four-story structure reflected in the windows of the building she was facing. The guide quickly turned to look behind her, but there was no such structure to cause the reflection. Defying explanation, she continued to see the unexplainable building while relating Gracie's tale. Later, when she perused a collection of historic photos of the Pulaski Hotel, she confirmed with a pale face that it was indeed the building she had seen while telling Gracie's story.

Sadly, Gracie is the only member of her family buried in Savannah. Her parents never got over their grief and eventually moved back to New England. When they passed away, they were buried there in the cold north, leaving Gracie all alone in Bonaventure. Some speculate that this is one of the reasons the little girl's ghost still lingers. It's in the Bonaventure Cemetery where Gracie is most often sighted and where many believe her spirit still lingers. Visitors have long reported seeing a little girl in a white dress, skipping around the cemetery or playing in the grass before vanishing into thin air.

The ghost of the girl is readily identified as Gracie by a careful comparison with the statue located at her grave site. Said to be stunningly accurate, it depicts young Gracie sitting with her right hand resting on the stump of a tree. There's now a wrought iron fence surrounding little Gracie's grave, and to this day it's constantly adorned with gifts, trinkets —but especially toys, stuffed animals and dolls, all left by visitors touched by Gracie and her story. Gracie also likes to play with coins, and it's said that if you place a quarter in the statue's hand and circle it three times, the coin will disappear.

As Christmas approaches, the number of toys left for Gracie seems to increase. Local legend says that if any of the toys are removed from the grave site, the statue will cry tears of blood, and the spirit of the little girl will follow the thief. The Savannah Historical Society says there are an estimated 28,000 people buried at Bonaventure, but Gracie's grave remains easily one of the most popular. Once in the cemetery you can find the exact location of Gracie's grave by checking in at the visitor's house. Go say hi, but be sure and bring a toy.

# The Dollhouse of Hope Hill Cemetery

Little Dorothy Marie Harvey was born February 4, 1926 and died June 1, 1931. She was the 5-year-old daughter of a family passing through Medina, Tennessee on their way up North in search of work. Dorothy had contracted the measles, and by the time the family arrived in Medina, she was far too weak to complete the rest of the journey. Sadly, she passed away there in Medina. Her devastated family had no funds to ship her body to their final destination, let alone pay for a proper funeral, so the townspeople of Medina generously donated the funds necessary to give the child the burial she deserved.

Dorothy Marie was laid to rest at Hope Hill, Medina's local

cemetery, and she still gathers lots of visitors. Even today, the young girl's grave draws in local residents and visitors – for the monument above her final resting spot is not your traditional grave marker. At the time of her death, many children's graves were marked with a lamb or cherubs as their markers, but Dorothy Marie was given much more. Rather than a tombstone, Little Dorothy Marie's marker is a tiny house filled with children's dolls and toys.

Visitors still leave toys for Dorothy, and there are many local stories claiming Dorothy still hangs around and loves the toys left by her visitors. Many leave crayons, drawings, dolls, and stuffed animals. However, the locals will tell you if you pay her a visit and do not leave a gift, she will express her disappointment by scratching or burning you.

One young man doubted the existence of little Dorothy and decided to test the sage warning. He visited her final resting place and purposefully left without leaving a gift. As he was driving away from the cemetery, he felt a burning sensation on his back. It wasn't until he got home that he discovered a child's handprint on his back, right where he'd felt the burning sensation, perhaps left behind as a torturous reminder for his disbelief or lack of generosity.

Those adventurous enough to take an evening stroll through the cemetery looking for the little girl's dollhouse often pull up and leave their cars running so their headlights illuminate a path. Again, if they don't leave a present for Dorothy, she will make herself known. Some even say she follows empty-handed visitors back to their cars, with the sounds of pitter-pattering footsteps behind them.

One group of curious visitors were startled when they made their way back to their car. The headlights suddenly switched off, leaving them stranded in complete darkness. As they rushed back in the dark, the headlights suddenly switched back on, blinding them all.

On one occasion, a woman entered the cemetery at night to pay a visit to the famous dollhouse. On her way there, she felt something push against her leg. When she peered down, she witnessed a ball of light shoot by and disappear behind a tombstone. Could this be Dorothy attempting to play a childish game or perhaps warning the woman to turn back and return with a present? Many witnesses claim to see a strange light emanating from the dollhouse; some even say they see the child playing with toys, while others have heard a little girl's laughter and even spoken words, as if she's attempting to chat with those passing by.

Chapter 4: Where Children & Spirits Play

If you ever have the opportunity to visit this cemetery on your own, please don't trespass or be disrespectful. But do look for the dollhouse, and when you find it, make sure to take a good look through the window all the way to the very back, for you just might get a glimpse of Dorothy looking back at you, as she patiently waits for her family to return.

Ferris, Stephen James, Artist, and Charles Dater Weldon.
Dream-land / painted by C.D. Weldon ; etched by S.J. Ferris. ©1883. Image.
Retrieved from the Library of Congress, https://www.loc.gov/item/97501308/.
(Accessed January 18, 2017.)

# The Forgotten Children

In what appears to be a normal suburban neighborhood on Beacon Hill in Seattle, Washington, is a lovely dog park. What might surprise you is that the idyllic setting isn't what it's always been. Where Fido can now romp around with other four-legged friends is actually sacred ground, the only hints of it's sacred past are the remnants of 20 tombstones scattered around the grounds.

It was on November 2nd (the Day of the Dead) in 1987 when the City of Seattle proceeded to bulldoze through what they claimed was no longer a cemetery, ripping up the existing tombstones. Rumor has it that as the cemetery fell into disrepair and neglect, the city began to sell it off bit by bit, erroneously claiming all the bodies at rest there were carefully moved elsewhere.

What most locals didn't know was the location was rich with interment history, predating white settlement of the area. Once traditional burial grounds for the Duwamish tribe it became known to local residents as "The Old Burial Grounds." The land was later acquired by the Maple Family in the early 1890s and used as a pioneer cemetery, and became the final resting place for a number of early

## Chapter 4: Where Children & Spirits Play

residents. In its prime, it is believed the cemetery held more than eight hundred graves. However, the land quickly filled up, and new burials stopped in the 1930s. The last recorded burial was a child named Jewel Lundin, who passed at three years of age on September 21, 1936.

Several houses were built over what was once the children's section of the cemetery, and current residents claim ghosts of children are living in their homes. One of these homes appeared on a local TV show, addressing the ghost problem that has haunted them for years.

Several families in the area have reported inexplicable happenings in their homes. In one case, a woman reportedly found the items of her doll collection moved, as if someone had been playing with them. Not entirely unexplainable at face value —until you realize she kept all of her dolls enclosed in a glass case. She claimed to find them lying on the floor or sitting in chairs throughout her home when she would wake in the mornings.

Another family's young boy was getting into trouble when he would repeatedly leave his toys on the floor time and time again, even though he adamantly claimed he had not touched the toys. The parents didn't believe him and continued to punish him. It wasn't until their son told them about a boy who would visit him in the night and sit at the edge of his bed that his parents realized something was beyond the ordinary. The son said the boy wore strange clothes and did not speak, but he believed the boy was there to watch over him.

Many of the resident children have seen ghosts from the cemetery grounds roaming through their disrupted resting place. A little boy has been seen by numerous witnesses running around the neighborhood only to vanish without a trace behind nearby trees. Witnesses also hear the laughter of children on the breeze late at night, when children should be in bed asleep. Mysterious lights will also appear and then suddenly disappear, and some say bushes and trees will shake, even when there is no wind or breeze.

Enjoy your stroll on Beacon Hill, but be mindful and respectful of where you tread.

## Playful Spirits of the Myrtles Plantation

Deep in the south in the state of Louisiana is the sleepy town of St. Francisville. Here lies one of the country's most well-known, pre-Civil War homes known as the Myrtles Plantation. The Myrtles is a classic antebellum plantation, built in 1796 by General David Bradford, leader of the Whisky Rebellion who fled to the then Spanish-controlled area to avoid prosecution for his role in the uprising. Approaching the site is like stepping way back in time. Towering live oak trees and a winding drive lead back to the impressive home. There's a brick courtyard and a 125'-long veranda with oversized rocking chairs that call out to visitors to sit back, cool off from the oppressive southern humidity and relax a spell.

Classic antebellum architecture and inviting spaces aside, there's another fascinating aspect to the Myrtles—it's considered to be one of the most haunted houses in all of the United States. The historic location has been featured on dozens of paranormal programs and is a popular "bucket list" destination for ghost hunters from all around the world.

It's hard to separate the rich history of the Myrtles from the countless stories and folktales that have been added to its mythology over the years. There are rumors that the home was built on top of an ancient Tunica Indian burial ground. Tourist information on the home says it was the site of no less than ten murders, and perhaps even more. Supposedly there are at least a dozen ghosts still haunting the plantation. Today The Myrtles is a popular bed and breakfast. It offers both historical tours and "mystery" tours that recount some of the many ghost stories associated with the impressive antebellum structure.

The spirits of children are frequently encountered at The Myrtles, both inside and out. Numerous people have witnessed the phantom of a little girl, peering out of one of the windows of the home. Some witnesses report that she even waves. Two young blonde girls have been spotted playing on the veranda, but always seem to fade away before anyone can capture a photograph. The two girls have also been encountered within the home, startling visitors by appearing suddenly, or standing at the foot of a guest's bed and then vanishing into thin air. Other visitors report a child spirit that likes to bounce on the beds. Tour guide Hester Eby has also seen the ghost of another little girl, following along nonchalantly with the rest of her tour-goers. When it dawned on Hester that there wasn't supposed to be a little girl in the tour group, she looked for the child only to discover she had inexplicably disappeared.

Many of the mansions rooms are named for former owners of the property or prominent figures somehow associated with the plantation. Among them is the second floor 'Fannie Williams' Room. It has a full-sized, half-tester bed and is fondly known as the "Doll Room," where spirits have been known to frequent.

The 'Ruffin-Stirling' Room is the home's former nursery. In it the spirits of children are said to play with items left out, causing them to disappear. They seem to have a particular fondness for lipstick and makeup, and the missing items often turn up under the bed. On the mantle periodically rests a porcelain doll that has been known to mysteriously vanish, only to reappear in its customary location later.

There's another doll on the mantelpiece in the 'William Winters' Room. It's an old rag doll that is purported to suddenly leap off the mantle and fly across the room. Sometimes it jumps up towards the room's chandelier. According to The Myrtles history, the room is where a young child died after a Voodoo priestess failed in an effort to try and save her.

Balls will roll across the floor in some of the rooms, apparently of their own accord, as if the ghostly hands of unseen children were pushing the balls back and forth between them.

One visitor to the home reported using a set of jacks as a trigger object after hearing the laughter of children late one night. The jacks were placed on the floor and soon after, they all vanished, never to be seen again by the visitor.

A man working at the plantation in the early 2000s reported a strange incident involving one of the porcelain dolls that sits on a bedroom mantle. One morning he saw one of The Myrtle's female guests downstairs and stopped to speak with her for a moment. He asked the woman where her young child was, and the woman replied that she was fine, but was sleeping upstairs in the stroller. The employee got very excited and told the woman she should not leave her child upstairs unattended. He rushed up the steps to check on the child and when he entered the room, there was the little one, asleep in the stroller, but standing next to the stroller was the doll from the mantle, one hand ominously resting on the side of the stroller. The man grabbed the child and rushed downstairs to report the incident.

Whatever spirits dwell at The Myrtles, many of them are playful and appear to be children with a love of toys and games. But others perhaps have a more unsettling nature. Visit and enjoy, but use caution, for there are strange things lurking about in the deep south.

Chapter 4: Where Children & Spirits Play

## Spooky Little Girl

Seattle might just surprise you on how truly haunted it is. Although a relatively young city and lacking the substantial history of its counterparts on the East Coast, it does have its fair share of ghosts.

In the heart of Pioneer Square is the Scheurman Building located at 102 Cherry Street. Built in 1890 after the great Seattle fire which destroyed most of the city, the building is known for its shady past. It was once home to a speakeasy, a haven for ladies of the night and a few other ventures of dubious legality. Today it's home to the Spooked in Seattle Ghost Tours, tucked away in the basement, with plenty of creepy hauntings for the curious. Numerous witnesses have seen a ghostly woman wandering around and calling out *"Are you there?"* over and over again, along with the shadow of what appears to be a man lurking in the darkness, apparently watching your every move. But the most well-known ghost is that of a little girl. Her name is unknown, but her presence is very much felt. In July of 2012, Spooked in Seattle Tours jumped on the opportunity to move into this hair-raising old place, an ideal location for their otherworldly pursuits. With brick arches, creaky doors and a musty smell, strange things began to happen almost immediately.

Prior to moving in the space had been sitting abandoned for more than two years. Before that, it was an Italian restaurant known as DeNunzio's. When Spooked in Seattle received the keys, they discovered an assortment of junk left behind by the previous owners. One object that stood out above the others was a child's wooden chair. Well worth keeping, the chair was moved to an empty room and the rest of the junk hauled out. Strangely, it seemed the chair would move about on its own, as if it was never in the spot it had been originally placed. Throughout the day, the chair seemed to move slowly across the room, and at one point, chalk circles were drawn around the legs just to prove the bizarre activity was indeed happening. And it truly was - right after the marks were made, the chair moved four feet when no one was looking! In the next few months, the chair would be found in various new locations throughout the room each morning. The staff began to look forward to finding its new location each morning when they opened for business.

When DeNunzio's occupied the space, the owner and workers talked about the spectral lingering of a little girl that skipped about giggling, and would be seen peeking around corners. One night after the restaurant closed, the staff heard the sounds of a child laughing. When they went to explore the noises, they were shocked to find dishes lying on the ground like a table setting, as if a child had been playing with them. Perhaps this same little girl was still occupying the space and moving the chair in the middle of the night? If there was a ghost of this child, then the current activity might be her way of letting the new owners know she was still around. So they got her a doll. This doll was dressed in period clothing with a music box inside of her. Shortly after placing the doll on the chair for the little girl, it wasn't too long until the doll would be found moved around the room as well. One night the doll was found propped up against the wall beside the chair. Another night, the doll would be lying on the church pews across the room, as if the doll was sleeping or laid down to a pretend nap by a child at play.

It was late one evening just after closing, when one of the owners was heading out the door to lock up, when the sound of the music box filled the staircase. Immediately he rushed down to investigate, only to find the music had stopped just as quickly as it started. From time to time, witnesses would catch snippets of the music box playing, but could never witness it occurring in real time, not until Spooked in Seattle had a paranormal investigation team catch the whole thing on video. In the recording you can clearly hear the music box playing as the team slowly crept up to the doll. The investigators were giddy with excitement, and one of the team members wanted everyone to be quiet so they could listen. He called out, "Hush!" Unfortunately, this seemingly urged the doll to stop as well. The video is now featured on one of their Pioneer Square tours.

Today, the spooky little girl makes herself known every so often. She seems to come out and play when there are other children present. You might find she has moved her doll as if to let the other children know they can play too, or you may hear the tiny music box call to you from the place she calls home.

Chapter 4: Where Children & Spirits Play

# Journey to the Island of the Dolls

Our boat moves calmly across the placid canal waters. The pace is slow, but in this part of the world, rushing through things seems to border on sinful behavior. The craft is called a "tranjineras," brightly painted in vibrant reds, yellows, green and white. It's a canoe-like vessel, propelled gondola style by a short Mexican man utilizing a pole to push us along the canal. The journey has taken two hours under the blazing sun of Mexico, but the destination is finally in sight. It's a small island buried deep in this region's complex canal system and the locals say it is haunted. It is known as La Isla de las Munecas. The Island of the Dolls.

A stillness fills the air as we approach the island. Even the water seems calmer than usual and the breeze is non-existent. There's a sense of anticipation and quiet excitement at finally reaching this strange destination, but there's something else, too. The place feels outside of reality, the very air gripped in the clutches of something unseen, something waiting and watching.

The boat pulls up to the island next to a shallow flight of steps that lead ashore.

You can feel eyes on you even before you leave the boat. They are watching from every direction. Hundreds, perhaps thousands of lifeless, artificial eyes on the dolls that populate the island. While their presence is obvious from the boat, once on land it is clear they dominate the landscape of this remote corner of Mexico.

They hang from the branches of every tree in sight, strung up with rusted metal wire, hanging by worn threads, and tucked into the branches of gnarled trees. Some have been in place so long nature has grown around them, causing weird marriages of root, vine and plastic. They can be seen upon the highest limbs, and scattered on the ground, staring up from the rich, wet soil. Some are missing limbs and are worn from their time spent under the unforgiving southern sun. Others look abused by the rain and time. Sometimes there's only the head of a doll, eyes wide, casting accusing glances at the island's latest intruders.

The dolls are said to be haunted, possessed by a spirit unable to find peace. This restless soul is forever destined to spend its time on the island, attempting to lure in those foolish enough to fall under the spell of the place.

The bizarre island's origins lie in the mysterious death of a young girl who perished in the canal, and with a man obsessed with appeasing her restless spirit.

In the 1940's, Don Julian Santana was a married man with a small family, living quietly in the coastal region of Mexico. No one knows why, but in 1950, Don Julian suddenly left his family and the world behind and moved to a small island deep in the canals south of Mexico City.

The island became Don Julian's home for the remaining fifty years of his life. He lived quietly for a time, taking trips to nearby port cities on a regular basis for supplies. He and his wife never divorced, though he only saw her and his children on rare occasions. He never invited his family or any friends to visit him on the island. It appears that Don Julian simply wanted to disconnect from the world and live out the rest of his days as a hermit.

Locals in the nearby cities all knew Don Julian and left him alone, exercising courtesy, and respecting his desire for privacy when he came into town. The reclusive man began to exhibit odd behavior, and locals became unnerved by his actions. Townspeople began to notice the hermit digging in trash heaps and garbage dumps when he came into port. Don Julian wasn't just scavenging for essentials though, he was looking for a particular item. Dolls.

The old man would make an effort to obtain dolls on each of his visits to the mainland and he started bringing things with him to barter. Often it was fresh fruits grown on his island, or other items he had acquired. He would offer what he had — in exchange for dolls. He didn't even care whether or not a doll was broken or missing pieces — it was only important he obtain as many as he could.

Eventually curiosity got the better of one of the residents and he asked Don Julian why he was so focused on collecting dolls. HIs response was both disturbing and compelling. Don Julian told the man his island was haunted by the ghost of a little girl who had drowned in the nearby canal system. The girl's spirit was taunting Don Julian, and the only way he believed he could appease her was by bringing her dolls and distracting her so she would no longer focus solely on him.

The story spread like wildfire in the closely-knit, agricultural region and the legend of the Island of the Dolls began.

Walking around the island is akin to a stroll in Wonderland.

## Chapter 4: Where Children & Spirits Play

Albeit a very bent, surreal version of Wonderland. It's doubtful even an anxious rabbit late for a very important date would be comfortable here with all the plastic eyes watching from every direction.

The dolls themselves are worn and tattered. Exotic spiders and other insects have made their homes in some of the countless plastic limbs and torsos. We strolled down a dirt path leading to the center of the island. Around a bend, a doll's head suddenly comes into view, half hidden by limbs and debris, its single eye staring with a life it shouldn't have.

It's hard to equate these strange decorations with living, breathing children. These toys are far from department store shelves, and most of them don't look like they should be dangling from the hands of playful little girls.

Legends say Don Julian would often fish dolls out of the canal. He believed they were sent by the spirit of the dead girl, a message to him that she was still very much present. He would promptly hang the dolls around the island in his bizarre tribute.

In keeping with tradition, we brought offerings with us for the restless soul. Our gift included candles, a handful of candy, and of course, a doll. All were purchased from local vendors when we hired the boat. The locals are more than willing to cater to those brave — or stupid enough— to come to this unusual place.

Using some twine, I hung the doll on a tree near the ramshackle shack at the center of the island. This was Don Julian's shelter and it seems a fitting place to leave the toy. Locals believe his spirit still resides on the island, watching over his peculiar creation, and forever trying to appease the spirit of the little girl.

We met a member of Don Julian's family working as a caretaker for the island. He welcomes visitors, shares stories, and of course, collects a small fee for the privilege of taking pictures of the location's famous residents.

He told us that Don Julian suddenly stopped going into town in 2001. It took a few of the locals some time to work up their courage, but eventually they made the trip out to the island to check up on the quirky old man. They found him lying dead in the water, in the same spot where the little girl had reportedly drowned all those decades ago.

While some believed the spirit had finally lured the hermit to a watery death, others insisted he was drowned by the possessed dolls themselves. Adding to the mystery, no cause of death has ever been listed for Don Julian, though many believe he simply had a heart attack.

*"There are many stories that tell why the dolls are here,"* the caretaker told us.

*"Some of the people believed that Don Julian was mad, but I don't believe that. When he first came to the island, he started to believe that the spirit of a young girl was here. She had drowned in the canal nearby and just after that he found the first doll floating in the water. He fished it out and tied it to a tree near the water to make the dead girl happy. He felt it would protect him from any evil. Soon, he felt that he had to add another doll, and another. It just never stopped."*

A number of television shows have filmed segments about the bizarre island. Popular travel host and food specialist Anthony Bourdain visited the location in 2008 while filming an episode of his show "No Reservations" while in Mexico City.

While Bourdain didn't witness any paranormal activity, he did speak with members of Don Julian's family who reported the elderly man had become depressed and physically ill due to his obsessive work in trying to appease the spirit of the deceased girl.

In 2009, Josh Gates and his "Destination Truth" crew journeyed to the island in the third season of the hit television show. The team spent the night on the island investigating various areas for ghostly activity. Gates and crew did encounter unexplained activity including EVPs, (electronic voice phenomena) unidentified thermal camera images, and strange noises. The team also documented a doll suddenly opening its eyes, seemingly in response to a comment made by Josh Gates.

The media attention the island has received has increased tourism to the creepy little spot. Travelers arrive on a regular basis now, bringing dolls to add to the ever growing collection. In time, these new additions will take on the weathered, grungy appearance of those already dwelling on the island.

Leaving the island had a strange effect. There's something that pulls at you, compelling you to stay. I asked our boat's pilot about coming back to the island at night, and what he thought about the population of creepy dolls dominating the landscape.

*"I won't go near the place after dark"* he insisted.

## Chapter 4: Where Children & Spirits Play

*"In the night, you can hear whispered voices, sometimes singing. The dolls talk to each other. They are possessed by restless spirits. They try to lure you in the darkness, hoping that you will drown. If you get close enough and if there is moonlight, you will see the dolls moving and you will see their eyes open and close."*

Indeed, my own recordings made while on the island contain strange sounds and whispers. Perhaps they are echoes of the restless souls of the little girl and the deceased caretaker attempting to make contact with the living.

The guide's comments echoed a common theme present in the stories about the island. People say the dolls move around at will, not bound by the wires and ropes that seemingly hold them in place. Walking around, there's always the sense that perhaps something just moved behind you, or just beyond the periphery of the corners of your vision. Is it the wind causing the effect, or something else?

Natural decomposition has added its touch to the bizarre gallery of grimy toys. Dolls are cracked and decayed. Some of the faces look agonized. Animals and insects have plucked at the false hair, often leaving only tufts sticking off to move in the wind. The sun has created blisters on plastic faces and over time, the rain has worn away the outer colors, leaving some dolls with a skeletal-like appearance.

Don Julian believed the voices of spirits wanted him to die. His constant fear drove him to create a landscape that looks like something from the mind of a mad man. But was the old hermit really insane?

In truth, it hardly matters whether or not the Island of the Dolls is genuinely haunted. It exists as one of the strangest locations on earth, created almost solely by one man's tormented mind. The symbols of his struggle to find peace hang from endless branches around the island. A reminder that left to dwell in a solitary world, the human mind can become fragile and delusional, or perhaps it opens up to a level of perception that few experience in our modern world.

Whether through madness or genius, Don Julian Santana created a legacy that will survive for many generations to come. The Island of the Dolls is a symbol both sad and strange. Those who choose to journey to it will find a portal to long forgotten memories, perhaps a spirit or two — but will no doubt stumble upon the ultimate collection — of Haunted Toys.

# About the Authors

## David Weatherly

David Weatherly has over 40 years of experience exploring the world of the strange, investigating the supernatural and examples of the paranormal around the world. He has written and lectured on a diverse range of topics including Hauntings, Cryptozoology, Ufology, psychic phenomena and ancient mysteries. David has also studied Shamanic traditions with elders from numerous cultures including Europe, Tibet, Native America and Africa.

David is a frequent guest on radio and television. His appearances include; History Channel's Ancient Aliens, Travel Channel's Mysteries at the National Parks, Gaiman TV's Beyond Belief and Coast to Coast

AM.

He is the author of several books including The Black Eyed Children and Strange Intruders. He is also the creator of the Wood Knocks series which focuses on Sasquatch.

For more information, visit:
http://twocrowsparanormal.blogspot.com/

# About the Authors

## Ross Allison

Ross Allison is a Paranormal investigator, author, media host, lecturer, teacher, tour guide and the Pacific Northwest's only full-time Ghost Hunter.

Ross is the President and Founder of A.G.H.O.S.T. (Advanced Ghost Hunters of Seattle-Tacoma). With close to 30 years of investigating the paranormal and over 16 years running a ghost hunting group, Ross travels internationally to investigate paranormal activity, collect ghost stories, research cemeteries and teach others about the strange things going on all around us.

Ross has been lecturing for Power Performers since 2004 and has spoken to thousands of students at hundreds of colleges and universities throughout the U.S. on his ghost hunting adventures and teaches a class based on his book, "Ghostology 101 – Becoming a Ghost Hunter" at the University of Washington and Tacoma Community College. His lectures have also taken him to such faraway locations as London, Canada and Scotland.

Through his travels he has had opportunities to work with some of the biggest names in the field, such as Jason & Grant of "Ghost Hunters" fame. He has also investigated some of the scariest and most haunted sites known to man, including the Stanley Hotel, Eastern State Prison, the Amityville House, Alcatraz Prison, Roman Catacombs, the Ancient Rams Inn and even the original location of "The Exorcist Case," where he captured some of the scariest phenomena ever encountered.

Ross is also the author of Ghostology 101, Spooked in Seattle, Tacoma's Haunted History, Hunted Historic Hotels, Psychology for the Ghost Hunter, Ghosts on Campus and Haunted Toys.

He's appeared on a number of radio programs, in magazines, books, news coverage and television shows, including The Learning Channel's America's Ghost Hunters, The Tonight Show, MTV, CMT, CNN, A&E, the Discovery Channel, ABC's Scariest Places on Earth, Sci-Fi's Ghost Hunters, Nightline, and two episodes of the Travel Channel's "Most Terrifying Places in America."

You may also find Ross wandering the streets of Seattle where he hosts the Spooked in Seattle Ghost Tours that takes guests to various haunted spots throughout the Seattle area.

For more information, visit:
http://spookedinseattle.squarespace.com/

Made in the USA
Lexington, KY
28 September 2019